PALERMO TRAVEL GUIDE 2023

Comprehensive guide to Palermo accommodation, when to visit, how to get around and travel planning 2023 and beyond

Monica J. Robbert

TABLE OF CONTENT

INTRODUCTION

P alermo, which is located on the beautiful island of Sicily, serves as a captivating entryway to Italy's extensive history and cultural legacy. This bustling city offers an enthralling fusion of influences from numerous civilizations that have influenced its character throughout the years, as evidenced by its centuries-old architecture, lively markets, and delectable cuisine. With its alluring blend of beauty and authenticity, Palermo beckons visitors with its majestic palaces and secret passageways.

Exploring the Historical Treasures of Palermo

You will be surrounded by a tapestry of architectural marvels as you meander through Palermo's serpentine alleyways. The Palermo Cathedral, the city's crowning achievement, exhibits a tasteful fusion of Norman, Gothic, and Baroque styles, representing the various influences that have influenced Sicily's history. The Palazzo dei Normanni, also known as the Royal Palace, lies nearby and enchants guests with its elaborate mosaics and lush gardens.

A magnificent example of Arab-Norman construction with beautiful Byzantine mosaics, the Capella Palatina is not to be missed.

Discovering Palermo's Cultural Attractions

Beyond its architectural splendors, Palermo has a rich cultural heritage. Ancient relics housed in the renowned Museo Archeologico Regionale provide insight into Sicily's former civilizations, notably the Greek and Phoenician. The Sicilian island's cultural heritage is displayed in the Galleria Regionale della Sicilia, which is home to a variety of Sicilian treasures.

The Delectable Cuisine of Palermo

Get ready for a unique gourmet experience with your taste buds. The cuisine of Palermo is a reflection of its multiethnic history. A feast for the senses, the lively street markets like Vucciria and Ballar provide mouthwatering displays of fresh food, fragrant spices, and regional specialties. Arancine (fried rice balls) and panelle (chickpea fritters), two of Palermo's most well-known street foods, should be tried.

Accommodations in Palermo

Palermo has a selection of lodging options to meet the demands of every visitor. There is a choice for every taste, from opulent boutique hotels housed in old structures to welcoming bed and breakfasts tucked away in picturesque areas. If you're looking for a little extra luxury, consider staying in one of the city's exquisite palazzos, where you can enjoy opulent amenities while taking in Palermo's rich history.

How to Navigate Palermo

The city well-connected transit system makes getting about reasonably simple. The city provides a robust network of buses and trams that make it easy to travel to the city's many areas and attractions. For those looking for a more private mode of transportation, taxis are also easily accessible. Alternatively, walking around Palermo is a fantastic way to experience the city's lively atmosphere and discover undiscovered jewels.

Geography and Climate

The environment offers a diversified landscape that begs travelers to explore its natural beauties, from its stunning shoreline to its alluring hills. This Sicilian gem offers a lovely setting for your journey along with a delightful Mediterranean environment. The magnificence of this Mediterranean paradise will be revealed as we explore the geography and climate of Palermo.

Geography

- The geographic setting of Palermo exhibits a beautiful fusion of highland splendors and coastal attractions. The city is situated on the Gulf of Palermo, whose coasts are encircled by the Tyrrhenian Sea. Sandy beaches like those in Mondello and Aspra beckon sun-seekers to soak up the warmth of the Mediterranean and partake in leisurely seaside pursuits. The summer months are the perfect time to relax in the sea's pristine waves.

Palermo is graced with rolling hills and attractive mountains that provide its landscape depth and character in addition to the city's allure from the coast. With its unmistakable silhouette, the Monte Pellegrino guards the city from above and offers breath-taking panoramic vistas. You'll come across lush valleys, lemon groves, and vineyards as you go farther inland, showcasing Sicily's agricultural richness.

Climate

- Palermo enjoys a typical Mediterranean climate with cool, rainy winters and warm, dry summers. The city has an amazing number of sunny days all year round, which fosters an enticing environment for leisurely outdoor exploration.

Palermo's main tourist season is from June through September during the summer. It's the perfect time of year to visit the beach and go sightseeing because the days are long and blessed with beautiful sunshine. The Mediterranean region's pleasant climate, with average temperatures in the mid-20s to low-30s Celsius (mid-70s to mid-90s F), welcomes you to relax.

- The months of spring (March to May) and fall (October to November) offer a more calm environment for exploring because of the milder weather and reduced visitors. These seasons are nice for outdoor activities and learning about different cultures because the typical temperature ranges from the mid-teens to the low 20s Celsius (mid-50s to low 70s degrees Fahrenheit) during these times.

- Compared to many other European cities, Palermo's winter (December to February) is still moderate. Temperatures normally remain in the mid-teens Celsius (low 60s F) throughout this time, despite the fact that rainfall is more frequent. The cultural offerings of Palermo, like as its historical buildings, museums, and festivals, can be enjoyed without the hectic throng throughout the winter.

Embrace Palermo's Natural Beauty

The topography and climate of Palermo make for the ideal setting for an unforgettable Sicilian journey. This Mediterranean paradise beckons you to discover its natural splendors, from sandy beaches to undulating hills. The topography and climate of Palermo create the ideal conditions for life-changing experiences, whether you choose to relax on sandy beaches, hike through stunning scenery, or explore the city's historical treasures.

As you set out on your journey, make sure you pack appropriately, taking the time of year and your intended activities into account. Accept Palermo's Mediterranean charms and allow its captivating location and temperate atmosphere to charm you at every turn.

Any traveler who experiences Palermo's intriguing fusion of history, culture, and cuisine is guaranteed to come away with a lifelong memory. This Sicilian jewel offers an immersive experience that will amaze visitors from near and far, from its stupendous architectural wonders to its delectable cuisine. Learn about Palermo's complex history, indulge in its mouthwatering cuisine, and appreciate the city's dynamic environment for a memorable voyage through time and culture.

History of Palermo

You will be strolling through the pages of history when you enter Palermo's maze-like streets. This thriving city has experienced the rise and fall of several civilizations, permanently altering its character. Palermo's historical story spans millennia, from its prehistoric roots to its medieval majesty and beyond.

Origins in the past and Phoenician influence

The name Palermo, which means "all-port" in Greek, dates back to antiquity when it was known as Panormos. Palermo, which was established by the Phoenicians in the eighth century BCE, swiftly developed into a significant Mediterranean trading center. The Phoenicians, who were skilled navigators, laid the foundation for the city's marine power, which would last throughout its history.

Roman and Greek Legacy

Palermo came under Greek rule in the fifth century BCE as the mighty city-state of Syracuse expanded its control across Sicily. Greek culture flourished during this time, and enormous temples were built, including the Temple of Heracles, which still exists as a reminder of Palermo's former glory.

Palermo went through a period of Roman influence when Sicily was conquered by the Romans in 254 BCE. Aqueducts, theaters, and opulent homes were all constructed by the Romans, who also left their mark on the city's infrastructure. Despite their dominance, Palermo preserved its distinctive identity and cultural legacy by fusing Roman traditions with its own particular customs.

A Prosperous Golden Age During Arab Rule

The Arab invasion brought in a period of affluence and cultural interaction, which in the 9th century marked a crucial turning point in Palermo's history. The city enjoyed a prosperous golden period when under Arab authority, developing into a thriving hub of learning and commerce. Muslim, Byzantine, and Jewish communities coexisted peacefully in Palermo as it developed into a multiracial metropolis.

The architecture of Palermo is especially influenced by the Arabs. During this time, the iconic Arab-Norman design, known for its elaborate geometric patterns and beautiful mosaics, achieved its pinnacle. Magnificent buildings like the Palazzo dei Normanni and the Capella Palatina serve as enthralling examples of the seamless blending of Arab and Norman architectural features.

Sicily's Kingdom and the Norman Dynasty

The Normans founded the Kingdom of Sicily in the eleventh century after taking control of Palermo. Palermo prospered as a hub of political, intellectual, and artistic influence during the Norman era. The city saw the development of imposing churches that combined Norman, Gothic, and Byzantine styles, such as the Palermo Cathedral.

Palermo gained notoriety for its lavish palaces and imposing cathedrals, which served as examples of the city's wealth and artistic prowess.

Beyond Baroque Splendor

Another wave of change to Palermo's architectural landscape occurred during the Baroque era. Intricately ornamented cathedrals and palaces were constructed, forever altering the appearance of the city. Palermo embraced the opulence of the Baroque style, resulting in an eye-catching display that still holds the attention of tourists today.

Modernity and Cultural Resurrection

Numerous historical occurrences, like as foreign invasions and governmental changes, have influenced Palermo's contemporary history. The city has undergone a resurgence in recent decades, regaining its cultural past and redefining itself as an exciting travel destination. Palermo's historic sites have undergone painstaking restoration, giving its medieval streets fresh life.

A Tapestry Of History Awaits

Explore Palermo's fascinating past as you travel among the ruins of the Phoenician, Greek, Roman, Arab, and Norman civilizations that intertwine to form a historical tapestry. Discover Palermo's archaeological wonders, where historic ruins and artifacts provide a window I nto bygone ages. Immerse yourself in the city's rich history while admiring the architectural wonders, such as the majestic Palazzo dei Normanni and the charming Capella Palatina.

The history of Palermo is not just found in its monuments; it also lives on in the city's thriving neighborhoods and regional customs. Explore the crowded markets like

Vucciria and Ballar, where the aroma of centuries-old trade is still detectable in the air. Engage the community to preserve Palermo's cultural history as they proudly uphold centuries-old traditions.

The story of the city's past also includes times of hardship and change. From invasions by foreign nations to social upheavals, Palermo has survived storms that have shaped its personality. However, it is because of these difficulties that Palermo has grown to be a strong city that captures the character of its citizens.

Palermo is a live reminder of its turbulent past today. It welcomes visitors to delve further into its history and embraces its multicultural roots and eclectic traditions. You'll be taken on a voyage that transcends time as you stroll through historic neighborhoods, indulge in authentic Sicilian food, or take part in exciting events that celebrate Palermo's rich cultural heritage.

Explore Palermo's streets, interact with its people, and embrace the city's ongoing legacy to learn more about its fascinating past. Palermo urges you to walk into its rich historical tale and experience the fascination of a city where history and culture meet, from the echoes of Phoenician commerce to the majesty of Norman conquerors and the tenacity of its people.

Traditions and Culture

It provides visitors with an enthralling trip into the heart of Sicilian heritage thanks to its numerous cultural influences and centuries-old traditions. The city's rich cultural tapestry is evidence of its turbulent past and the fortitude of its residents. Palermo's rich cultural tapestry weaves together an enthralling variety of traditions that are still practiced today, from expressive art forms to cherished rituals.

Expressions of the Arts and Festivals

Palermo is awash in art, which reflects the artistic character of the city. From historic treasures to modern works, museums, galleries, and even street corners are home to artistic expressions. Visitors are mesmerized by the accomplished creations of renowned artists at the Galleria

Regionale della Sicilia, which has an extraordinary collection of Sicilian artwork. Explore your local art scene to find hidden jewels, from modern art galleries to colorful street murals that breathe life into the city.

The calendar of Palermo is studded with colorful events honoring a tapestry of customs. A notable occasion is the city's patron saint Santa Rosalia's Feast, when residents line the streets with processions, music, and fireworks. Settimana Santa, or the Festival of the Holy Week, is a solemn celebration marked by centuries-old religious processions. The heart and spirit of Palermo's traditions can be seen via these cultural festivities.

A Heritage of Culinary Arts

The culinary scene in Palermo is a feast for the senses, steeped in tradition and shaped by the eclectic heritage of the city. Sicilian food tempts the palate with a mix of flavors by fusing the freshest regional ingredients with influences from the Arabic, Greek, and Norman cultures. Investigate the lively street markets in places like Vucciria and Ballar, where the fragrances of herbs, spices, and recently caught fish fill the air.

Enjoy traditional Sicilian meals like cannoli (crisp pastry filled with creamy ricotta), caponata (savory eggplant dish), and pasta con le sarde (pasta with sardines). The symphony of tastes that characterize Palermo's culinary legacy can be experienced when you pair your meal with a glass of Marsala wine made in the surrounding region.

The Hospitality of Palermo's Citizens

Warmth and hospitality of its citizens are woven into the cultural fabric of Palermo. Locals, known as Palermitani, are proud of their city's past and ready to teach visitors about their customs. Talking with the locals will provide a plethora of anecdotes, legends, and folklore that will help you understand the city better.

Palermo's culture is one of hospitality, and it's not unusual for strangers to be treated like family. Enjoy traditional fare, engage in spirited conversation, and immerse yourself in the dynamic atmosphere of Palermo as you embrace the friendliness of the locals.

Keeping Palermo's History Alive

Passionate people and organizations committed to upholding its traditions protect Palermo's cultural legacy. The preservation of Palermo's historical structures, the revival of ancient trades, and the support of regional craftspeople all contribute to the city's thriving legacy.

Traditional pottery, complex lacework, and fine goldsmithing are painstakingly created by artisans using age-old methods that have been handed down through the years. Discover the city's many artisan studios and shops, and bring a piece of Palermo's cultural heritage home with you.

Take in the Cultural Tapestry of Palermo

Immerse yourself in Palermo's diverse cultural heritage as you tour the city. Visit art galleries and museums to savor Sicilian tastes, admire artistic treasures, and experience the friendliness of the locals. Participate in the city's exciting festivities to feel the fervor of centuries-old customs come to life. Observe the enthusiasm of Palermo's citizens as they celebrate their heritage via vibrant processions, music, dancing, and delectable cuisine.

Investigate the local way of life in order to comprehend Palermo's culture and traditions on a deeper level. Learn how to make traditional Sicilian dishes using age-old recipes that have been passed down through the years by enrolling in a cooking class. You can learn more about Palermo's cultural subtleties and the principles that guide its residents by conversing with Palermitani in neighborhood cafés and trattorias.

Don't pass up the chance to take part in Palermo's vibrant street life. Enjoy a leisurely passeggiata along the charming waterfront promenade as you take in the energetic atmosphere of the city. Discover the tucked-away corners of the old marketplaces, where street performers, artists, and merchants weave a tapestry of sights and sounds that capture the vibrant spirit of Palermo.

The cultural history of Palermo is not just restricted to the past; it is a dynamic force that accepts contemporary inspirations while firmly rooted in tradition. Contemporary art exhibits, music festivals, and theatrical productions give national and international artists a platform to express themselves and add to the cultural history of the city.

The traditions and culture of Palermo are an essential component of the city's identity, defining its personality and capturing the hearts of travelers. Take advantage of the chance to become fully immersed in Palermo's cultural tapestry to better comprehend its past, its people, and the unique character of this fascinating city where tradition and modernity coexist.

CHARACTER 1

Planning Your Trip to Palermo

An exciting journey loaded with historical marvels, a dynamic culture, and culinary treats awaits travelers who set out for Palermo. In order to guarantee a great encounter, careful planning is essential. The following are some crucial pointers to help you organize your trip to the heart of Sicilian grandeur.

Best Time to Visit Palermo

Palermo attracts tourists all year round with its alluring fusion of historical marvels and vibrant culture. The best time to visit this Sicilian treasure is crucial for making the most of your trip and experiencing Palermo in all its glory. Here's a look at the changing seasons that provide an unforgettable voyage through the alluring world of Palermo.

April through June in Spring: Embracing Mildness and Holiday Spirit

In the embrace of spring, Palermo blooms as winter bids adieu and nature awakens. The months of April to June include pleasant weather, rich scenery, and less tourists. The main tourist season is over, so now is a great time to visit the city's architectural wonders, like the Palermo Cathedral and the Palazzo dei Normanni, without the crowds.

Additionally, Palermo celebrates in a vivacious way during the spring. During celebrations like the Feast of Santa Rosalia, when processions, music, and fireworks illuminate the streets, you may fully immerse yourself in the city's rich cultural tapestry. Discover the friendliness of the inhabitants as they celebrate their long-standing customs, fostering a lively and joyful atmosphere.

From July to September, enjoy the festival season and sunny bliss
Between July and September, Palermo has its most alluring season. The city comes alive with a variety of cultural events and a contagious sense of enthusiasm as the temperatures rise. Palermo's most vibrant celebrations, such

as the Festival of the Holy Week (Settimana Santa) and the Feast of Santa Rosalia, are held around this time.

Long, bright days make it possible to explore Palermo's historical buildings at your own pace, while the city's outdoor atmosphere is best enjoyed in the evenings. Passeggiate with the locals along the waterfront promenade, savor outdoor cuisine at buzzing street cafés, or just relax on the city's stunning beaches.

October to November: Embracing Mildness and Harvest Delights in Fall

Palermo offers a beautiful fusion of good weather and abundant harvests as summer gives way to October. Discovering the city's cultural riches in October and November is a great opportunity to avoid the summertime throng. Palermo's historical landmarks and neighborhoods can be explored comfortably while the temperature is still mild.

Take advantage of the wealth of fresh vegetables produced by autumn harvests by indulging in the flavors of Sicilian cuisine during this time. As you set out on a gastronomic trip through Palermo's streets, sample local specialties, visit neighborhood markets, and take in the essence of Sicilian culinary traditions.

Palermo's Eternal Allure

Despite the fact that each season has its own unique appeal, Palermo's everlasting attractiveness is unaffected by the calendar. Visitors are nevertheless enthralled by the city's rich history, cultural legacy, and warm welcome even in the winter, when temperatures drop and showers may be more frequent.

Anytime you decide to visit, Palermo will be happy to have you. Every time you choose to explore Palermo's enchanting streets, you are invited to go on a journey through Sicilian grandeur, from the bright spring festivities to the sun-drenched bliss of summer and the harvest delights of October.

Pick Your Moment to Discover Palermo's Magic

Choose the season that aligns with your preferences and set out on a tour through the alluring world of Palermo. Take in the beauty of this Sicilian jewel as you explore its fascinating past, indulge in its delectable cuisine, and become immersed in the lively local culture. Whatever time you decide to visit Palermo, it is waiting for you and eager to show you its magic.

How to reach Palermo

Arriving in Sicily's vivacious metropolis of Palermo marks the beginning of an incredible journey. Travelers from all over the world are drawn to this Mediterranean gem because of its rich history, cultural richness, and culinary delights. Here is a guide to assist you choose the best mode of transportation and start your adventure to the fascinating world of Palermo.

By Air

Falcone-Borsellino Airport (PMO), which is about 32 kilometers west of the city center, serves Palermo. The airport serves as a handy entrance point for travelers with its extensive domestic and international airline options. There are numerous airlines that offer connections to Palermo from major European cities and other locations.

There are many alternatives for ground transportation upon arrival. To get to your lodging in the city center or elsewhere, taxis are easily accessible outside the terminal. For a smoother journey, think about scheduling a private shuttle in advance or using ride-sharing services.

By Sea

Arriving in Palermo by boat offers a charming experience for those looking for a distinctive and attractive entrance. Ferries and cruise ships are welcomed in the Port of Palermo, which links the city to a number of Mediterranean locations. For those looking for convenient ways to tour Sicily by sea, ferry services from the Italian mainland, such as those from Naples, Genoa, and Livorno, are available.

After disembarking, you can easily commute to your desired location in Palermo thanks to the taxis and local transit that are conveniently located close to the port.

By Train

Excellent rail links between Palermo and other Italian cities allow for a beautiful trip across Sicily's countryside. Regular train service is provided to Palermo from important Italian towns like Rome, Naples, and Milan by Trenitalia, the country's national railroad corporation. The train ride offers a chance to take in Sicily's breathtaking coastal scenery and mountainous landscape.

You can easily access local buses, cabs, and trams at Palermo's Stazione Centrale, which is in the center of the city, so that you can travel farther into the neighboring areas or get to your desired location within Palermo.

By Road

The road network provides an easy way to get to Palermo for people starting a road trip adventure or arriving from nearby locations. Sicily's highways link the city to different regions of the island, offering picturesque landscapes and the freedom to travel at your own speed.

Major car rental agencies offer locations in Palermo and at the airport, enabling you to pick up a vehicle as soon as you arrive. Remember to educate yourself with local traffic laws and take into account the traffic situation during times of high travel demand.

Palermo's Transportation System and On-Foot Exploration

Getting about Palermo is simple once you get there. Taxis, trams, and other local transportation options offer convenient ways to get around and explore the city's attractions. While taxis provide a handy door-to-door service, buses and trams run regular routes connecting major sites and districts.

The small, walkable city core of Palermo is ideal for exploration. Explore the marketplaces, take in the ambience of the winding streets, and welcome the chance encounters that are waiting around every bend.

Start Your Palermo Adventure now

Reaching Palermo is simply the start of an amazing adventure into Sicilian grandeur with the variety of transportation alternatives at your disposal. Regardless of how you get there—by air, sea, train, or road—you'll be welcomed by a city bursting with gastronomic, cultural, and historical treasures.

As you tour Palermo's historical monuments, savor Sicilian food, and interact with the friendly residents, give yourself permission to become engrossed in the city's vibrant atmosphere. Spend some time organizing your travel and being familiar with your alternatives to ensure a smooth arrival and practical exploration of the city.

Remember to appreciate the impromptuness and fortuitous moments that make travel so unforgettable as you set out on your Palermo trip. Discover hidden treasures, get lost in the intriguing streets, and let Palermo's soul lead you to its timeless wonders.

Palermo is waiting for you, eager to capture your senses and reveal the splendor of Sicily, whether you arrive by air, sea, train, or road. So gather your belongings, start your adventure, and watch the enchantment of Palermo come to life.

Palermo's transportation system

Palermo, the vivacious capital of Sicily, has a variety of effective and convenient transit choices, making getting about a breeze. Palermo can accommodate your needs whether you value the ease of public transportation or the adaptability of private transportation. Here is a guide to help you get around the city and enjoy your time in Sicily to the   most

.

Take Public Transportation and Enjoy the Local Rhythm

Palermo has an excellent public transportation infrastructure that makes it simple to get throughout the city and its surrounds. The primary public transportation options in the city are buses and trams, which provide thorough coverage of all the neighborhoods and tourist hotspots.

Get on one of the city's buses to travel to well-known destinations including the Palermo Cathedral, the Teatro Massimo, and the Quattro Canti. The city's buses operate on a network of routes. The trams, with their charmingly retro appeal, are a fun way to travel through the city's streets while taking in the scenery.

Purchase tickets from the driver when you board or from specified kiosks. To save money and simplify your transit experience, take into account purchasing a multi-day or multi-ride pass. Plan your trips taking into account that bus and tram timings can change.

Taxis are practical and comfortable
In Palermo, taxis are an easy and pleasant way to get around, especially for quick journeys or when you need door-to-door service. You can either hail a cab on the street or find taxi stands all across the city.

In Palermo, authorized taxis are normally white and have a "TAXI" symbol on the roof. To ensure fair pricing, make sure the meter is turned on before you leave. If you'd rather, you can book a cab through your lodging or by utilizing one of the city's well-liked ride-hailing applications.

Taxis are a flexible alternative that let you customize your travel to meet your individual requirements, whether you're going to a museum, a restaurant, or a beach outside of the city.

Walking Around: Enjoy Palermo's Charm

Walking around Palermo's charming streets is one of the most enjoyable ways to discover the city. The city is the perfect place for leisurely strolls and unplanned discoveries due to its small size and pedestrian-friendly areas.

Explore the old center, where you'll find stunning buildings, evocative squares, and quaint passageways around every corner. Spend some time exploring the lively marketplaces, such the Ballar Market or the Vucciria, where Palermo's odors, sounds, and hues come to life.

Always wear comfortable shoes and follow the local rhythm when traveling by foot. Engage the amiable natives, who are always happy to offer advice or tell tales about their cherished city.

Using a rental car to travel outside of Palermo

Renting a car provides the utmost freedom and flexibility if you want to travel outside of Palermo and take your time discovering the picturesque cities and landscapes of Sicily. Palermo is home to several car rental companies, some of which have locations right at the airport, making it simple to pick up and return your vehicle.

To drive safely through Palermo's streets, you must be conversant with the city's traffic laws and driving restrictions. Remember that parking might be difficult in some areas, especially in the city center, therefore it is best to use paid parking lots or ask about parking options at your lodging.

Discover Palermo's Treasures Easily

Assuring that you can easily discover the city's historical beauties, revel in its gastronomic delights, and immerse yourself in its vibrant culture, Palermo's transportation system is made to enrich your Sicilian trip.

Palermo has a variety of mobility options to fit your interests, whether you decide to embrace the rhythm of public transportation, enjoy the convenience of taxis, embrace the charm of exploring on foot, or select the independence of a vehicle rental.

Pick the form of transportation that best suits your schedule and level of preferred convenience. As you board a bus or tram and enter Palermo's daily bustle, embrace the local rhythm. Enjoy the ease and comfort of taxis as they take you to your selected locations, offering a stress-free method of city navigation. Utilize Palermo's small size and friendliness to pedestrians by strolling through its charming streets to take in the atmosphere and discover hidden gems. Alternately, you might hire a car to travel outside of Palermo and explore Sicily's breathtaking scenery and quaint towns at your own time.

Embrace the adventure and let Palermo's vivacious spirit lead you as you travel the city. Consult the locals, who are renowned for their friendliness and kindness, to learn about local experiences and hidden gems.

To truly appreciate all that Palermo has to offer, remember to arrange your transportation in advance, become familiar with the timetables and routes, and allow enough time. Navigating Palermo's charming streets will surely improve your trip to Sicily, whether you go by public transportation, taxi, walking, or a combination of these methods.

By embracing the transit alternatives that best fit your travel needs, you may easily uncover Palermo's hidden gems and begin an exciting adventure of this alluring Sicilian city.

Entry requirements and Visa

You must be aware of the entry and visa formalities before traveling to Palermo, the alluring capital of Sicily. Here is a guide to assist you in completing the required steps so you can enter Palermo's realm of Mediterranean grandeur without incident.

Obtaining a Visa

It's crucial to know whether you need a visa to visit Italy or Sicily before embarking on your Palermo vacation. Depending on your country of origin, intended use for visiting, and length of stay, different visas may be required.

Italy follows standard visa procedures because it is a member of the Schengen Area.

For visits of up to 90 days during a 180-day period, visitors from a wide range of nations—including the United States, Canada, the United Kingdom, Australia, and the majority of member states of the European Union—can enter Italy without a visa. However, it is always advised to check with the Italian embassy or consulate in your country of residence regarding the precise visa requirements based on your nationality.

You must apply for the proper visa in advance if you intend to stay in Palermo or Sicily for a lengthier time than the visa-free period or for activities like job, study, or family reunion. Make sure to give yourself enough time before your intended trip for the visa application process.

Documents to Facilitate Your Arrival Requirement
It is crucial to have all the required documentation in order in order to guarantee a smooth entry into Palermo. The following are the main criteria to think about:

- Valid Passport: Verify that your passport is still valid at least six months after the date you intend to leave Italy. This need is true for Palermo as well as the majority of other overseas travel locations.

- Obtaining a Schengen visa before your trip is a must if you need one to enter Italy or Sicily. At the border crossing, provide your passport and visa.

- Having proof of your lodging in Palermo is important. Examples include hotel bookings or a letter of invitation if you're staying with family or friends.

- Carry documentation showing you have the money you need to support yourself while visiting Palermo. Bank statements, credit card statements, and traveler's checks are examples of this.

- Proof of Return/Onward Travel: To prove your intention to depart Italy within the allowed time frame, it is advised to have a return or onward travel ticket.

- Travel insurance: Having travel insurance that covers medical costs, trip cancellation, and other unforeseen occurrences is strongly advised, however it is not a required.

It is important to understand that border control officials may decide to inquire about extra paperwork or information in order to determine your eligibility for admission. To ensure a simple entry into Palermo, it is usually advisable to be well-prepared with complete travel documents.

Start Your Sicilian Adventure now

You may guarantee a trouble-free trip to this fascinating city by being familiar with the visa and entry procedures for Palermo. Verify the individual rules based on your nationality, gather the required paperwork, and, if necessary, give yourself plenty of time for visa processing.

Prepare to give yourself over to Palermo's alluring beauty, extensive past, and thriving culture when you arrive there. Spend time learning about the customs of the area, savor some delicious Sicilian food, and let the people of Palermo warmly welcome you to their Mediterranean paradise.

Having satisfied all entry and visa formalities, you may confidently begin your Sicilian trip. As you experience Palermo's historical wonders, savor its gastronomic pleasures, and make lifelong memories in the heart of Sicily, let its seduction capture your senses.

Keep an eye on your passport and other travel documents while you are in Palermo. Keep them secure—ideally in a hotel safe—and carry backup photocopies or digital copies. Upon arriving, it's also a good idea to register with your embassy or consulate so they can help you if something happens.

If you intend to go outside of Palermo to other regions of Sicily or Italy, be sure to adhere to any additional entrance or visa restrictions that may apply. Prior to your journey, it's always advisable to be informed and current on any changes to visa requirements or entry requirements.

Keep in mind that visa and entry requirements may change based on the reason for your trip, your nationality, and the length of your stay. Therefore, it is imperative to confirm the precise laws that apply to your circumstance in advance.

Let Palermo's breathtaking architecture, bustling markets, and balmy Mediterranean breeze transport you into a world of cultural delights as soon as you step foot there. Explore the city's fascinating past, savor its delectable cuisine, and interact with the welcoming inhabitants who personify Palermo.

As you explore the wonders of this alluring Sicilian city, Palermo, may your voyage there be one of enchantment and discovery.

Exchange of money and currency

It's crucial to become familiar with the local currency and possibilities for exchanging money before beginning your journey to Palermo, Sicily's cultural center. You may confidently browse Palermo's markets, stores, and restaurants if you are aware of the financial environment. To ensure a smooth financial transaction, refer to this guide about Palermo's currencies and money exchange.

Accepting the Euro as a currency

Italy, including Palermo, uses the Euro (EUR) as its official currency. Italy joined the European Union and made the Euro the only form of legal money, streamlining trade and fostering continental economic unification. This implies that the majority of your purchases in Palermo will require you to have Euros on hand.

How to Get Euros: Your Exchange Options

You can choose from a number of practical alternatives to obtain euros for your trip to Palermo:

Currency Exchange Offices

- Palermo has many currency exchange offices, especially in popular tourist locations, airports, and significant train stations. These businesses provide the option to exchange your local currency for euros. Remember that conversion rates and costs might differ between exchange offices, so it's best to compare prices and find out if there are any additional fees before completing the transaction.

Banks

- Palermo banks can help you exchange currencies. They typically offer rates that are competitive, and some might even have special currency exchange offices for handling international transactions. It is important to keep in mind that banks have set business hours, typically from Monday to Friday, and may be closed on weekends and federal holidays. Plan your currency exchange accordingly as a result.

Automated Teller Machines (ATMs)

- There are common sight in Palermo and offer a practical way to withdraw euros from your bank account. ATMs can be found in banks, airports, retail malls, and other busy areas, and they often offer cheap exchange rates. Inform your bank of your travel intentions before you depart to make sure your debit or credit card will function abroad. You should check with your bank to learn about any applicable fees or withdrawal limitations because some ATMs may charge withdrawal fees.

Credit and debit cards

- They are generally accepted in Palermo, particularly in hotels, fine dining venues, and bigger businesses. Carrying a large international credit card or a card with a well-known payment network (like Visa or Mastercard) is advised. Convenience, security, and favorable exchange rates are all provided by credit cards. However, it's wise to keep some cash on hand in case a card isn't accepted at a larger establishment, a local market, or in other circumstances.

Traveler's checks

- Although they used to be a common way to exchange money, traveler's checks have become less used in recent years. They may still be accepted by some banks and exchange offices, but they can be more difficult to cash and may have greater fees than other options. For enhanced convenience, it is advised to carry additional payment methods like cash or credit cards.

The Financial Advice

Keep the following helpful advice in mind as you visit Palermo's markets, shops, and restaurants:

1. Learn what your country's currency currently exchanges for against the euro. You can estimate the value of the goods and prevent any misunderstandings during transactions if you do this.

2. For increased flexibility, accept a variety of payment options, including cash and credit cards. This makes sure

you're ready for a variety of circumstances and businesses that can have varied payment preferences.

3. To prevent any problems using your credit card overseas, let your bank or credit card company know about your vacation intentions. Ask whether there are any additional fees or foreign transaction costs for using your card in Palermo.

4. Bring smaller Euro denominations with you for convenience, particularly when dealing with smaller companies, street sellers, or public transportation when precise change could be needed.

5. Use a tight money belt or a disguised wallet to protect your cash and valuables. To avoid theft or pickpocketing occurrences, be aware of your surroundings, especially in crowded places.

6. Your credit card information, including the card number and the bank's contact information, should be kept in a safe

place. In the event that a card is lost or stolen, this will be useful.

7. Make a plan for your currency exchange and make sure you have enough euros on hand to cover your expected costs. For convenience, it's a good idea to carry both larger and smaller bills.

8. To ensure fair prices and reduce the risk of counterfeit currency, look for reputed currency exchange companies or banks. Never exchange money with unauthorized people or street vendors.

9. Think about utilizing one of the increasingly popular digital wallets or mobile payment apps in Palermo, such Apple Pay or Google Pay. To find out if your mobile payment methods are appropriate for overseas purchases, check with your bank or card issuer.

Accept the financial tapestry of Palermo

You can easily navigate Palermo's financial environment by being familiar with the city's available currencies and methods of currency exchange. If you want to fully immerse yourself in Palermo's captivating experiences, make sure you have the necessary Euros by considering the ease and security provided by banks, currency exchange companies, ATMs, and credit/debit cards.

Allow Palermo's historic alleyways, bustling markets, and delectable cuisine to enchant you as you begin your Sicilian experience. Take advantage of the chance to revel in the local culture, create lasting purchases, and enjoy Sicily's distinctive cuisine. If you have a firm grasp of Palermo's money exchange and currency, you may set out on your journey with financial assurance and discover the wonders of this alluring city.

CHAPTER 2

Top Attractions in Palermo

A wide variety of prominent attractions that highlight the city's storied past and vibrant present are sprinkled across this Mediterranean jewel. Explore Palermo's intriguing world as we introduce you to some of the city's most recognizable sights and cultural treasures.

Cathedral of Palermo

The magnificent Palermo Cathedral (Cattedrale di Palermo) is located in the center of Palermo, amidst the city's busy streets and vibrant marketplaces. This remarkable architectural marvel provides a window into Sicily's rich cultural tapestry and occupies a distinct place in the history of the city. As you enter the revered spaces of Palermo Cathedral, where centuries of art, faith, and architectural brilliance have intertwined, you will embark on a trip through time.

An Array of Architectural Forms

The Palermo Cathedral is a standing example of the city's rich history and many different architectural influences. The cathedral was initially built in the 12th century, but has experienced various changes over the centuries, creating an eclectic blend of styles. The cathedral's facade, with its solid stone walls and massive bell tower, clearly shows the Norman influence.

The Gothic portal's elaborate decorations and graceful arches will welcome you as you approach the entryway. When you go inside, the beauty is revealed to you. The interior displays the historical layers that have built Palermo's cultural scene with a tasteful fusion of Gothic, Baroque, and Neoclassical components.

Incredible Treasures Inside

A treasure trove of artistic and theological marvels can be found inside Palermo Cathedral, mesmerizing guests with their beauty and historical importance. Admire the stunningly detailed mosaics that adorn the central nave and represent biblical themes and saints. The city's artistic heritage is evidenced by these mosaics with Byzantine influences that date to the 12th and 13th centuries.

Explore the cathedral's interior space deeper to find the Chapel of the Holy Sacrament, a magnificent example of Baroque architecture. The chapel exudes an ethereal beauty because to its superb stucco work and golden ornaments. The elaborate graves of Sicilian kings and queens, which pay homage to the island's former rulers, further enhance the cathedral's regal atmosphere.

The Exceptional Treasury

Without visiting the magnificent treasure, a trip to the Palermo Cathedral is not complete. You'll find a variety of priceless items and holy artifacts here that demonstrate the richness and piety of earlier generations. Admire finely carved reliquaries made of gold and silver, jeweled chalices, and vintage books, each of which has a unique tale to tell. The Pala d'Oro, a golden altarpiece set with priceless diamonds, and the Crown of Constance of Aragon, a marvel of medieval goldsmithing, are two of the treasure's highlights.

Accept the Glory of the Palermo Cathedral

The Palermo Cathedral is a tribute to the city's continuing spiritual and cultural legacy as well as a beacon of Palermo's architectural heritage. Discover its beautiful halls, be amazed by its works of art, and let the echoes of history direct your steps.

Palermo Cathedral guarantees an outstanding experience that will make a lasting effect on your tour through Palermo's charming streets, whether you are an art fan, a history buff, or a curious traveler wishing to immerse yourself in Sicily's enthralling past.

Teatro Massimo

At the majestic opera theater in Palermo's Teatro Massimo, a genuine jewel of Sicilian culture, immerse yourself in the world of performing arts. Teatro Massimo stands as a tribute to Palermo's ongoing love of music and theater with its spectacular neoclassical architecture, lavish interiors, and a rich history of enthralling performances. Step into this wonder of architecture and allow the entrancing music and spellbinding performances to carry you away to a realm   of   creative   genius

A Neoclassical Architectural Wonder

The remarkable example of neoclassical architecture, Teatro Massimo, is located in the center of Palermo. The theater's facade, which dates to the late 19th century and displays a tasteful fusion of Doric, Ionic, and Corinthian columns, exudes a sense of grandeur and classical beauty. The towering front, which is embellished with sculptures and fine details, gives a glimpse as to the creative riches that await inside.

A Tour of the Cultural Heritage of Palermo

Entering the revered spaces of Teatro Massimo places you in a space where creative prowess and cultural legacy meet. Visitors are in awe of the theater's opulent and meticulously designed interiors. Admire the beautiful chandeliers, elaborate ceilings, and plush velvet seating that have been painstakingly created to enhance the audience's experience and evoke a sense of grandeur.

Attractive Acoustics and Performances

Opera, ballet, symphony concerts, and theatrical plays are just a few of the world-class performances that have made Teatro Massimo famous. The theater's stage has hosted the abilities of great performers from throughout the world, from orchestras and artists of the past to those of the present.

The theater's outstanding acoustics, which have been meticulously designed to assure the best sound quality, are one of its most prominent features. The resounding sound of opera singers' powerful voices filling the huge hall is a really remarkable experience.

Guide Tours: Behind the Scenes

In addition to its enthralling shows, Teatro Massimo gives visitors the chance to peek behind-the-scenes magic. Visitors are led on a tour of the backstage spaces, learning about the technical components of theater production and getting a glimpse into the performers' daily lives. Explore the rehearsal spaces, take in the elaborate stage mechanics, and walk out onto the legendary stage where countless performers have written history.

Accept the Magnificence of Art

Palermo's persistent commitment to the performing arts is demonstrated through Teatro Massimo. As you enter this architectural wonder, immerse yourself in the worlds of music, drama, and dance. The Teatro Massimo welcomes you to appreciate the creative magnificence that has mesmerized audiences for more than a century, whether you attend a spellbinding performance, take a guided tour, or simply awe at the majesty of the theater's interiors.

Quattro Canti

The stunning Quattro Canti (Four Corners), located in the midst of Palermo's historic district, are a remarkable example of the Baroque beauty of the city. This magnificent square, a work of architecture, functions as a bustling intersection where Palermo's spirit comes to life. Quattro Canti welcomes you to immerse yourself in the enthralling splendor of Palermo's past. It is decorated with elaborate fountains, statues, and exquisite structures.

Stunning Baroque Architecture

Famous architect Giulio Lasso created Quattro Canti, a symmetrical square that masterfully combines art and urban design, in the 17th century. The Via Maqueda and Corso Vittorio Emanuele converge at the area, making it a busy center of activity for Palermo.

You'll be enthralled by Quattro Canti's complex design as soon as you arrive. Four nearly identical Baroque facades that each symbolize a different historic area of the city adorn the square. The facades are embellished with magnificent statues, allegorical figures, and balconies that show off the period's superb craftsmanship.

Storytelling and Symbolism in Stone

Quattro Canti is a stunning architectural ensemble that also serves as a visual historical and cultural account of Palermo. The statues and ornaments that adorn the façade are representations of significant people, saints, and symbols that help to portray the city's story.

Look at the statues of the four Spanish monarchs, Philip II, Philip III, Philip IV, and Charles V, which are prominently displayed at the corners and represent Palermo's Baroque period loyalty to the Spanish throne. Admire the delicate carvings of the cherubs, personifications of Palermo's great characteristics, and representations of the four seasons.

A Lively Palermo Crossroads

Quattro Canti is more than simply a charming plaza; it is a bustling intersection where bustle is constant day and night. The area serves as a gathering place for both locals and tourists, providing a lively atmosphere where modernity and antiquity mix. As you stroll the nearby streets, take in the vibrancy of Palermo as lively markets, chic shops, and classic trattorias tempt your senses.

The Enticing Glory of Quattro Canti

Palermo's Quattro Canti neighborhood is a unique architectural gem, fusing the energy of the city with Baroque elegance. Spend some time admiring the fine details, taking in the lively ambiance, and appreciating the creativity that has defined Palermo's personality as you stroll through this charming square. Let Quattro Canti take you back in time while continuing to be a dynamic representation of Palermo's tenacious character.

Palazzo dei Normanni

The Palazzo dei Normanni (Palace of the Normans), which is tucked away among Palermo's busy streets, stands as a magnificent tribute to the city's extensive historical past. This magnificent palace invites tourists to follow in the footprints of kings and queens with its alluring architecture and magnificence. Discover the tales that have created Palermo's fascinating past as you explore the luxurious halls that are filled with gorgeous mosaics and magnificent artwork.

A Palace With a Rich History

The Palazzo dei Normanni, which was initially constructed as a stronghold during the Arab era, underwent substantial changes under the Norman kings who conquered Sicily in the 11th century. One of Palermo's most notable architectural icons, it now serves as the location of the Sicilian Regional Assembly.

Arab influences and grand architecture

A fascinating architectural fusion that displays elements from several historical eras may be seen in the Palazzo dei Normanni. By embellishing the ancient Arab building with ornate elements, the Norman rulers put their stamp. The Palatine Chapel, a masterwork of Arab-Norman art, is the palace's most outstanding architectural feature.

Palatine Chapel: A Gem of Arab-Norman Art

Prepare to be transported to a realm of unmatched beauty as soon as you enter the Palatine Chapel. The chapel combines aspects of Byzantine, Arab, and Norman artistic traditions in its complex mosaics, delicate stucco work, and captivating gold leaf accents. Observe the Old and New Testament scenes that have been painstakingly crafted and colorfully portrayed on the chapel's walls and ceiling.

The King's Hall and Royal Apartments

Make your way through the magnificent Royal Apartments as you tour the Palazzo dei Normanni. These chambers provide an insight into the rich lifestyle of Sicilian royalty thanks to its ornate furnishings, frescoes, and priceless tapestries. Stand in amazement in the Hall of Kings, where Sicilian kings and queens were crowned, and allow your thoughts to roam amid the echoes of their regal rituals.

Santa Maria degli Angeli Chapel

Don't miss the Chapel of Santa Maria degli Angeli in the royal complex, a tranquil haven with tasteful frescoes and a calming ambiance. Take a minute to escape the splendor of the palace by entering this small area and absorbing its spiritual atmosphere.

Palazzo dei Normanni unveils Palermo's past

Palermo's historic grandeur and the blending of various cultures that have defined the city's identity are symbolized by the Palazzo dei Normanni. Walk in the steps of Sicilian kings and queens as you explore its regal halls, take in the stunning artwork, and sense the weight of history. If you enjoy history, art, or simply want to learn more about Palermo's rich heritage, a trip to the Palazzo dei Normanni is guaranteed to be a memorable trip through time.

Market Ballaro

Experience the sensory joys of Palermo's Ballar Market, a thriving and busy commercial center. This bustling market provides an enthralling look into Palermo's way of life and culinary traditions. It is filled with a kaleidoscope of colors, heady fragrances, and the animated conversation of vendors. Enter Ballar Market's colorful tapestry to start your culinary journey, which will tease your taste buds and stimulate your senses.

A Fusion of Gastronomic Delights

The Ballar Market is a representation of the rich cultural history and varied culinary influences of Palermo. This ancient market has long been a gathering place for people and traders, fusing aromas and ingredients from Sicilian, Arab, and Mediterranean cultures.

The Feast of the Senses

Fresh vegetables, fragrant spices, and regional specialties will meet you as you make your way through the Ballar Market's congested alleyways. Let the eye-catching hues of fruits and vegetables, from ripe tomatoes and citrus fruits to aromatic herbs and leafy greens, capture your attention. Allow the aroma of hot bread, salty cheeses, and cured meats to fill the air and tempt you to taste their mouthwatering aromas.

The Gastronomic Treasures of Palermo

Ballar Market is a treasure trove of Palermo's culinary treats, not just a place to buy ingredients. Taste the legendary Palermo street cuisine, like the panelle (chickpea fritters), arancini (fried rice balls), and the delicious pani ca meusa sandwiches made with spleen. Enjoy the freshest seafood, with sellers showcasing their day's catch with pride. Taste some of the handmade cheeses, olives, and regional treats that highlight the complex flavors of Sicilian cuisine.

Cultural Experience

Ballar Market provides a fascinating look into Palermo's daily life and culture in addition to its thriving food scene. Interact with the welcoming sellers, who are always willing to share tales, recipes, and tidbits about their wares. Watch the locals' animated conversations as they barter for the greatest deals and trade rumors. The dynamic ambiance of the market and the variety of its patrons provide a mash-up of cultures and a microcosm of Palermo's vibrant character.

Take Advantage of Ballaro Market's Flavors

A location where flavors, scents, and traditions converge to produce a dynamic and alluring experience, Ballar Market is a culinary treasure trove. Discover the maze-like lanes, indulge in the delectable street food, and embrace the diverse cultural influences that have defined Palermo's cuisine. Ballar Market guarantees an immersive and fascinating tour through Palermo's culinary environment, whether you're a devoted foodie, a curious traveler, or an avid photographer documenting the market's vivid sceneries.

Hidden Gems & Off the Beaten Path Locations

Beyond the well-known sights, Palermo is home to a treasure trove of undiscovered sites that are just waiting to be discovered. These lesser-known gems provide a distinct and genuine window into the city's essence, enabling adventurous visitors to stray off the beaten path and learn about Palermo's best-kept secrets. Enter the magical realm of Palermo's hidden gems by setting out on an adventure journey.

San Lorenzo Oratorio: A Baroque Gem

The Oratorio di San Lorenzo, a hidden gem that takes tourists to the splendor of Baroque art and architecture, is tucked away in a peaceful area of Palermo's historic center. This modest yet intriguing oratory features stunning murals, delicate stucco work, and a beautiful ceiling covered in minute details. The elaborate magnificence that awaits within will enchant you as you enter; it is a monument to Palermo's rich creative legacy.

A Journey into the Macabre: Catacombe dei Cappuccini

The Catacombe dei Cappuccini offers a hauntingly singular experience for those who enjoy the macabre. These catacombs, which are located beneath the Capuchin convent, contain the well preserved mummified remains of Palermo's wealthy people. Explore dimly lit passageways lined with rows of elaborately attired mummies, each with a unique tale to tell. This undiscovered treasure offers a fascinating, albeit gloomy, look at Palermo's burial customs and preservation techniques.

Vucciria Market: A Gastronomic Journey

Enter Vucciria Market to experience the lively bustle and sensory overload of sights, sounds, and smells. This vibrant market, which is situated in the old Kalsa neighborhood, provides a genuine glimpse into Palermo's culinary tradition. Explore the booths stocked with tasty spices, vibrant fruits and veggies, and fresh seafood. Engage the vivacious merchants, who would be happy to tell you about their experiences and lure you with samples of their mouthwatering wares. Let your sense of taste lead you through this secret gourmet haven.

A Miniature Wonderland: Stanze al Genio

Stanze al Genio is a jewel that shouldn't be missed by art lovers. This unusual museum presents an astonishing collection of intarsia, or Sicilian marquetry, hidden away in a private property. Be in awe of the minute wooden inlays' deft artistry as they adorn the furniture, walls, and ceilings, weaving a spellbinding visual tapestry. The dedicated curator will lead you through this hidden realm of art so that you can appreciate the minute particulars and important historical context of each work.

Discover Palermo's Secret Treasures

The hidden treasures of Palermo provide a sense of exploration and a deeper appreciation for the city's rich tapestry of artistic, historical, and gastronomic traditions. Entertain yourself in Palermo's lesser-known wonders by setting out on a tour off the beaten path. These hidden gems, which include elegant oratories, scary tombs, lively marketplaces, and small art, allow you to discover

Palermo's mysteries and make lifelong memories. As you explore the off-the-beaten-path marvels, let curiosity be your guide.

Walking Tours In Palermo

Walking about Palermo is a satisfying and engaging experience that lets you interact with the city's vivacious soul and uncover its fascinating stories. Walking tours provide an intimate experience through Palermo's rich history, architectural wonders, and local gems, from the twisting lanes of the old center to the secret corners filled with charm. Put on your walking shoes and set off on a guided tour to experience Palermo's soul step by step.

Learning about the Historic Center

Start your walking tour in the ancient core of Palermo, where a plethora of architectural marvels are waiting for you. Wander through the confusing lanes of the Kalsa neighborhood, which was once a bustling Arab neighborhood, and be amazed at the blending of Arab, Norman, and Baroque elements. Discover the Quattro

Canti, a beautiful square with ornate statues and facades representing the city's historic areas. Take a moment to savor Palermo Cathedral's splendor and explore the tales that have created this famous structure.

Markets of Palermo exploration

Without stopping at one of the city's vibrant markets, no walking tour of Palermo is complete. In Ballar Market, where the aromas of fresh vegetables and sizzling street cuisine fill the air, follow your guide through the bustling kiosks. Get to know the vivacious sellers, discover the fresh ingredients, and savor the tastes that characterize Palermo's culinary scene. The markets are a feast for the senses and a window into city life, from the delicious street food treats to the vibrant displays of local goods.

Disclosing Secret Treasures

Allow your guide to show Palermo's hidden gems as you veer off the usual path. Discover the fascinating Oratorio di San Lorenzo, a Baroque treasure hidden in a peaceful nook. Intricate Sicilian marquetry is on display in the private museum Stanze al Genio, where exceptional craftsmanship is on display.

Find out about the spooky Catacombe dei Cappuccini, where mummified remains rest. These undiscovered treasures offer a greater comprehension of Palermo's cultural legacy and give an insight into some of its lesser-known tales.

Taking a Walk Along the Waterfront

A leisurely stroll along Palermo's waterfront, where the sea breeze and breathtaking vistas create a tranquil ambiance, is a relaxing way to cap up your walking tour. Take in the magnificence of the marina and the imposing Teatro Massimo, one of the biggest opera houses in Europe. Stop at the waterfront's attractive piazzas and squares where folks congregate to chat and take in the beauty of their city.

Immerse Yourself in Palermo's Soul

In Palermo, walking tours offer more than just a chance to take in the sights; they also give visitors a close encounter with the city's spirit. Allow yourself to be led through its winding streets, listen to the history spoken by the historic structures, and take in the colorful tapestry of daily life.

You'll gradually unearth the layers of history, culture, and tradition that contribute to Palermo's allure. So, lace up your walking shoes, widen your senses, and set off on a journey that will help you gain a better understanding of Palermo's undiscovered attractions.

Gardens and Parks

E scape Palermo's busy streets and spend some time in the city's serene parks and gardens, where tranquility and nature abound. These verdant havens invite people to unwind, relax, and connect with the natural beauty of their surroundings as a refuge from the metropolitan tumult. Explore the rich marvels of Palermo's parks and gardens, where colorful blossoms, tranquil retreats, and beautiful landscapes await.

Villa Giulia: A Haven for Botanicals
Enter the magical world of Villa Giulia, a vast park that mesmerizes with its colorful flora and natural beauty. This expertly maintained garden, which is close to the ocean, has a large range of plants, including exotic species and traditional Mediterranean flora.

Take a leisurely stroll along the twisting trails, take in the aromatic air, and find quiet nooks. Villa Giulia provides the ideal getaway into the embrace of nature, from the vibrant flowers of the flower beds to the shadow of towering trees.

A horticultural delight: Palermo's Orto Botanico
The Orto Botanico di Palermo is a must-visit location for anyone who enjoy the outdoors and plants. This botanical garden, which opened its doors in 1789, is a veritable

encyclopedia of botanical marvels. Explore its well-kept lawns, take in the variety of plants and flowers, and immerse yourself in the knowledge and research that are being conducted there.

A haven for biodiversity, the Orto Botanico di Palermo is home to rare species, healing herbs, and exotic plants that coexist peacefully.

A Royal Retreat: Parco della Favorita

Escape to the gorgeous park known as Parco della Favorita, which emanates regal splendor. This vast park, which was once a hunting preserve for the Bourbon royalty, is decorated with classy roads, rich greenery, and a regal palace. Take in the tranquil atmosphere and the breath-taking vistas of the surrounding scenery as you stroll or ride a bike leisurely around the park's tree-lined paths. The Parco della Favorita is a peaceful refuge where history and nature coexist.

A Haven with English influences: Giardino Inglese

Experience the allure of the Giardino Inglese, a garden with English influences that takes you back in time. This picture-perfect park offers a tranquil ambiance and lovely views. It is decorated with statues, fountains, and winding walks. Take a leisurely stroll over the immaculate lawns, find refuge under the towering trees, or locate a secluded bench to indulge in some quiet time. A hidden treasure, the Giardino Inglese is a place where harmony with nature reigns supreme.

Welcome the Serenade of Nature

The parks and gardens of Palermo provide a pleasant haven of tranquility and unspoiled beauty apart from the bustling activity of the city. These green areas beg you to relax, reconnect with nature, and revitalize your senses, whether you're looking for vivacious blooms, horticultural wonders, regal retreats, or the elegance of an English garden.

So go for a leisurely stroll, find a quiet place to read a book, or just enjoy Palermo's parks and gardens; a calming symphony of tranquility is waiting.

CHAPTER 3

Palermo's Neighborhoods

T he city of Palermo is home to a variety of neighborhoods, each with its own special charm. These areas, which combine centuries of history, culture, and everyday life, show off Palermo's diversity from the city's bustling fringes to its ancient core. Explore Palermo's neighborhoods and learn about the unique characteristics that make each one a fascinating place in its own right.

District of Kalsa

Learn about the fascination of Kalsa, one of Palermo's most charming neighborhoods that is tucked away in the city's historic core. Kalsa, which is steeped in history and has been inspired by many different cultures, provides a singular fusion of architectural marvels, artistic riches, and a buzzing contemporary atmosphere. Get lost in the textured streets and squares of Kalsa, where the past and present collide to produce an extraordinary experience.

A Tour of Human History

- You will be taken back in time to the time of Arab control and the rule of the Norman rulers as you stroll through Kalsa's twisting streets. This area was previously Palermo's thriving Arab neighborhood, distinguished by its winding lanes, secret courtyards, and elaborate buildings. Admire the surviving examples of this era's architecture, such as the palatial arches of Palazzo Abatellis and the San Francesco d'Assisi Church's embellishments with Arabic influences.

Baroque Glamour

- Additionally, Kalsa is home to a wide variety of spectacular Baroque structures that showcase the thriving artistic era of the city. Admire the Palazzo Chiaramonte-Steri's elaborate façades and ornate decorations. This building served as the Spanish Inquisition's former headquarters. Spend a minute admiring the magnificence of the Palazzo Mirto, a magnificent aristocratic home that provides a window into the luxurious way of life of the past. These architectural marvels serve as evidence of Palermo's creative past and cultural diversity.

Splendid Piazza Kalsa

- Kalsa's bustling central square, Piazza Kalsa, is always alive with activity. Historic structures adorn this bustling gathering spot, notably the majestic Palazzo Steri, which houses the University of Palermo's Rectorate. Enjoy a leisurely stroll around the area while taking in the ambience as inhabitants go about their daily lives while sipping a cool beverage at one of the outdoor cafes. The ideal location to experience the genuine atmosphere of the neighborhood is Piazza Kalsa.

Artist Communities

- In addition, Kalsa has developed into a bustling hub for modern art and culture that draws both professionals in the field and art fans. Discover the cutting-edge exhibits at the Palazzo Riso, a museum of modern art housed in a former convent from the 17th century. See the thriving art culture that thrives within Kalsa's historic walls as you discover independent galleries showing the works of up-and-coming artists. This neighborhood is a hub for artistic expression where innovation and tradition converge.

-

Embrace Kalsa's Charm

- The district of Kalsa in Palermo is a must-visit because of its distinctive fusion of history, art, and local life. Explore the past, be in awe of the architectural marvels, and embrace the thriving current scene that exists there. Allow yourself to be enchanted by Kalsa's beautiful ambiance, where the pulse of contemporary Palermo blends with the echoes of the past.

District of Albergheria

Discover the Albergheria neighborhood in Palermo's historic center and its timeless charm. Albergheria offers a look into the city's colorful past and immerses tourists in a world of history and charm with its maze-like streets, historic churches, and architectural marvels. Discover hidden courtyards, get lost in the little lanes, and find the hidden gems that make Albergheria such a memorable place.

A History's Tapestry

- The history of Albergheria is rich, reflecting the numerous civilizations that have impacted Palermo throughout the ages. Take a stroll around its cobblestone streets and take in the architectural marvels from various eras. Admire the magnificent Byzantine mosaics of the Palatine Chapel, which were created by Norman and Arab artists. Discover the magnificent Palermo Cathedral, a magnificent building that combines Norman, Gothic, and Baroque characteristics. These well-known sites serve as evidence of Albergheria's historical importance.

Beautiful Squares and Piazzas

- Charming piazzas and squares can be found all across Albergheria, where locals and guests congregate to mingle, unwind, and take in the scenery. Visit Piazza Bellini, a charming plaza surrounded by medieval structures and the antiquated remains of a Roman villa. Spend a few minutes relaxing under the spectacular Fontana Pretoria, a lavish Renaissance fountain embellished with legendary sculptures. In the midst of the busy streets, these lovely areas offer a calm haven that invites you to appreciate Albergheria's splendor.

Religious Tradition

- Numerous churches and other places of worship may be found in Albergheria, showcasing the city's rich spiritual tradition. Visit the Church of San Cataldo, which features distinctive red domes and is a rare example of Arab-Norman architecture. Enter the Martorana, also known as the Church of Santa Maria dell'Ammiraglio, and be enchanted by the magnificent mosaics. These holy places not only include stunning artwork but also provide a window into Palermo's intricate religious past.

Local Culture and Food

- You will see the lively rhythm of local life taking shape as you explore Albergheria. Wander past quaint cafés where the aroma of cappuccino and freshly baked pastries fills the air, as well as busy markets and traditional businesses. Enjoy the flavors of Palermo's cuisine while trying arancini, panelle, and cannoli, three of the city's most popular street foods. The Albergheria district offers a true flavor of Palermo's thriving food culture by bringing the city's culinary traditions to life.

Enter Albergheria's Eternal Beauty

- With its timeless beauty, Albergheria beckons you to meander through its ancient alleyways, see its architectural wonders, and enjoy the area's rich cultural legacy. Spend some time getting lost in the maze of alleyways, stop to take in the elaborate facades, and let the history wash over you. The Albergheria neighborhood offers a fascinating journey through time and an amazing experience to anybody who visits. It captures the spirit of Palermo's history.

District of La Vucciria

Enter the vibrant La Vucciria neighborhood for a feast for the senses that combines vibrant views, alluring fragrances, and the bustling energy of the street food scene. The colorful market stalls, mouthwatering culinary options, and traditional Sicilian charm of this ancient area of Palermo have attracted both locals and tourists for years. Get lost in La Vucciria's culinary treats and lively ambiance as you set out on a unique culinary journey.

A Market Abundant in Life

The thriving market bearing that name is located in the center of La Vucciria. Here, the aromas of sizzling street cuisine, fragrant spices, and fresh produce fill the air. Wander around the winding streets where sellers proudly display their colorful assortment of fruits, vegetables, meats, seafood, and regional delicacies. Engage the vivacious sellers, who are always willing to provide their wisdom, tales, and suggestions. The market's contagious energy creates a bustling ambiance that perfectly depicts Palermo's culinary culture.

Roadside Food Paradise

La Vucciria is well-known for being a street food haven where you can savor a delectable variety of Sicilian specialties. Discover your favorite street foods at every turn as you make your way through the maze of vendors by using your senses to guide you. Arancini are golden-fried rice balls with tasty contents like ragù, cheese, or spinach. Sample panelle, which are crispy outside and delicate within chickpea fritters.

Don't forget to indulge in the sweet delights of cannoli, which are filled with creamy ricotta cream inside of crisp pastry shells. These tempting delicacies are just a sample of the delectable treats La Vucciria has to offer.

Genuine Sicilian tastes

La Vucciria is a treasure trove of authentic Sicilian ingredients and flavors in addition to being a place for street cuisine. Discover the freshest local food at the market's vendors, including ripe tomatoes, fragrant herbs, and delectable citrus fruits. Let the smells of handmade cheeses and olive oil from nearby sources lure you in. Also, try some of the delectable cured meats, including salami and prosciutto, which highlight the butchers of Palermo's artistic craftsmanship. Sicilian cuisine is built on these natural elements, which provide a true flavour of the region's culinary heritage.

Cultural Experience

Beyond its delicious food, La Vucciria is a historically and culturally rich area. Walk about Palermo and take in the colorful street art that adorns the walls, demonstrating the artists' inventiveness and freedom of expression. Investigate the nearby alleys where historic structures and secret courtyards emerge, revealing themselves and whispering tales of the past. Beyond the market, La Vucciria's spirit permeates the entire neighborhood with an air of sincerity and local pride.

Immerse Yourself with La Vucciria's Dynamic Ambiance

La Vucciria is a district that awakens the senses and enthralls both foodies and culture seekers with a vivid and immersive experience. Get lost in the crowded market, enjoy the flavors of genuine Sicilian street cuisine, and soak up the vibrant ambiance permeating the area. La Vucciria is a gourmet sanctuary that invites you to partake in a truly unique culinary trip by bringing to life the rich traditions of Palermo's food culture.

Mondello

E scape the hustle and bustle of the city and take in Mondello, Palermo's favorite beach neighborhood. Mondello, a coastal refuge with golden sand beaches, turquoise waters, and a bustling promenade, is nestled on the Tyrrhenian Sea's crystal-clear waters. Mondello offers visitors of all ages an amazing coastal vacation, whether they are looking for sun-soaked leisure, thrilling water sports, or a taste of the local food.

Beach Lovers' Heaven

One of Sicily's most attractive beaches, Mondello attracts both locals and tourists with its breathtaking natural beauty. As you soak up the warm Mediterranean sun, dig your toes into the fine, golden sand. Feel your worries melt away with each soft wave as you take a refreshing dip in the crystal-clear, turquoise waters. Families and swimmers of all abilities will enjoy Mondello Beach's shallow depths and quiet tides. Enjoy a refreshing beverage while lying on a sun lounger and taking in the breathtaking splendor of this coastal haven.

Aquatic Activities and Adventure

Mondello provides a variety of water sports and activities to get your heart pounding for those looking for a little extra adventure. Take a kayak or paddleboard and explore the coast at your own speed. Explore the ocean's depths to find a vibrant underwater environment filled with marine life. Sail or windsurf through the shimmering waves and feel the wind in your hair.

Mondello is a popular destination for lovers of water sports and outdoor adventures due to its favorable winds and good weather.

The Lovely Promenade

The picturesque promenade in Mondello, called "Via Regina Elena," is the ideal location for a leisurely stroll. The promenade has an aura of elegance and leisure because it is lined with beautiful Art Nouveau mansions and palm trees. Enjoy the exuberant atmosphere as locals and guests assemble to take in the seaside environment while taking in panoramic views of the beach and watching sailboats bobbing in the distance. Enjoy a delicious gelato or a cool granita while you bask in the sunshine and take in Mondello's distinctive seaside charm.

A Culinary Delight

Mondello is a culinary utopia in addition to a haven for sun and surf. Numerous beachside cafes, restaurants, and kiosks serving delectable Sicilian cuisine can be found along the promenade and sprinkled around the neighborhood. Enjoy exquisite pasta meals, freshly caught fish, and delectable pastries and desserts. Don't pass up the chance to taste the regional speciality "pani ca meusa," a sandwich filled with fried spleen and ricotta cheese that can surprise and entice daring cuisine lovers. The culinary scene in Mondello offers a delicious blend of tastes that properly accentuates the seaside setting.

A Seaside Retreat Near Palermo

Mondello, a peaceful oasis offering a soothing getaway from daily life, is a short distance from Palermo's downtown. Mondello is certain to create a lasting impression whether you spend the day relaxing on the beach, discovering the colorful underwater environment, or enjoying Sicilian cuisine. This beach area is a tribute to Palermo's varied charms with its natural beauty, inviting waves, and laid-back ambiance and a piece of paradise just waiting for your discovery.

CHAPTER 4

Dining and Nightlife in Palermo

The lively food scene in Palermo is a reflection of the city's varied cultural influences and long history. The dining options in Palermo are a gourmet feast for food lovers, with everything from classic Sicilian delicacies to creative fusion creations. As the sun sets, the city comes to life with a thriving nightlife that offers a variety of hip clubs, live music venues, and evocative enterprises where residents and guests can unwind and experience Palermo's vibrant character.

The Culinary Scene in Palermo

The robust culinary scene in Palermo is a reflection of the city's multifaceted cultural heritage and long history. Palermo offers a gastronomic trip that enthralls the senses and makes a lasting impact on food connoisseurs, ranging from classic Sicilian cuisine to cutting-edge culinary inventions.

Sicilian Specialties and Delicious Street Food

Palermo is well known for its Sicilian specialties, which honor the area's plethora of natural resources and age-old recipes. Enjoy arancini, the famous golden-fried rice balls filled with delicious ingredients like ragù, cheese, or spinach.

Get a taste of panelle, delicious chickpea fritters with a crispy outside and a delicate, savory inside. Enjoy the flavorful pasta alla Norma, a Sicilian meal made with ricotta salata, basil, tomatoes, and eggplant. Don't forget to indulge in a cannoli, a renowned Sicilian pastry filled with rich ricotta cream, to satisfy your taste buds.

Markets that are active and local produce

The vibrant marketplaces of Palermo, such Ballar and Vucciria, are a feast for the senses. Discover the colorful stalls stocked to the brim with a wide selection of fresh vegetables, flavorful herbs and spices, and locally sourced goods. Engage the amiable merchants, who are eager to impart their expertise and enthusiasm for their wares. These markets provide a special chance to experience the genuine flavors of Palermo, from ripe tomatoes and fragrant citrus fruits to handmade cheeses and cured meats.

Old-fashioned Pastries and Cute Cafés

Step inside the city's lovely cafés and ancient pasticcerias to experience Palermo's café culture. These cherished businesses have been enticing locals with their mouthwatering pastries, cakes, and aromatic coffees for years. Enjoy the cannoli's delicate sweetness, the marzipan's almond flavor, or the flaky richness of the cassata.

Enjoy your sweet delicacy with a cup of freshly brewed espresso or treat yourself to a flavorful granita, a semi-frozen dessert. The pasticcerias and cafés of Palermo offer a moment of relaxation and a taste of the city's age-old customs.

Fusion cuisine And modern cuisine

A thriving culinary sector that values innovation and fusion is also present in Palermo. Traditional Sicilian flavors have been reinterpreted by creative restaurateurs and chefs by fusing them with global influences and modern cooking methods. Take part in a gastronomic adventure that challenges perceptions and delights the palate. Palermo provides a wide variety of dining options for those seeking a distinctive and unforgettable gourmet experience, from Michelin-starred restaurants to contemporary eateries.

Food Festivals and culinary events

Palermo holds a number of food festivals and culinary events all year long to highlight the city's culinary excellence. Participate in the celebrations of the "Sagra del Pesce," a festival honoring the riches of the sea with a variety of seafood delicacies.

Investigate the "Cous Cous Fest," which showcases the diverse influences on Sicilian cuisine and includes a competition between chefs from other nations. These occasions provide you the chance to sample a variety of sensations and become fully immersed in Palermo's thriving culinary scene.

Prepare for a Culinary Journey

The culinary culture in Palermo is vibrant, diversified, and steeped in history, just like the city itself. Palermo offers a gourmet trip that satisfies both the daring and the purist, with ancient recipes passed down through generations and modern inventions that push the boundaries of cuisine. Set off on a culinary adventure and indulge your sense of taste.

Sicilian cuisine at its best

The dynamic capital of Sicily, Palermo, is home to a wealth of mouthwatering traditional Sicilian delicacies that honor the area's illustrious culinary past. Palermo's cuisine, which has been influenced by a confluence of cultures throughout history, is a reflection of the city's vivacious past and varied cultural influences. These traditional Sicilian treats offer a delicious trip into the flavors of Palermo, from robust pasta dishes to decadent sweets.

Arancini : Crispy Rice Delights

- Golden-fried rice balls known as arancini are a favorite street snack in Palermo that both locals and tourists adore. Arancini are stuffed with a range of savory ingredients such ragù (meat sauce), mozzarella, peas, and risotto flavored with saffron and are made with Arborio or Carnaroli rice. With the crispy crust serving as a pleasant counterpoint to the rich, creamy interior, each bite bursts with flavor. Arancini are a must-try treat in Palermo, whether they are consumed as a quick snack or as a component of a meal.

Pasta Norma: A Sicilian Classic

- The iconic pasta dish from Sicily, known as pasta alla Norma, was created in Catania but has since made its way to Palermo's culinary scene. In this delectable vegetarian dish, al dente pasta typically rigatoni or spaghetti—is combined with sautéed eggplant, sweet tomato sauce, fresh basil, and a substantial amount of salty, crumbly ricotta salata. Pasta alla Norma's exquisite symphony of flavors and textures beautifully illustrates the simplicity and depth of Sicilian cuisine.

Caponata :Sicily's Sweet and Sour Delight

- The distinctive flavors of Sicilian cuisine are best exemplified by the sweet and sour vegetable stew known as caponata. The ingredients in this well-known meal include eggplant, tomatoes, celery, onions, capers, olives, and vinegar, which are all perfectly cooked and given a sweet touch to create a delicious balance of flavors. Caponata can be eaten as a vegetarian main course, as a garnish for bruschetta, or even as a side dish. It is an authentic example of Sicilian culinary expertise thanks to its complex flavor and brilliant hues.

A Sweet Symphony: Cassata

- Cassata is a typical dessert from Palermo that must be sampled in order to be fully experienced. Layers of liqueur-soaked sponge cake, sweetened ricotta cheese, candied fruit, and a marzipan coating make up this famous Sicilian confection. Cassata is a treat for the eyes as well as the palate thanks to its aesthetically pleasing look, which is frequently covered with vibrant frosting and elaborate motifs. Each mouthful is a symphony of tastes and textures that displays the skill and craftsmanship of Sicilian pastry baking.

Brioche And Granita: A Refreshing Pair

- Locals and visitors to Palermo look for cooling treats like granita and brioche on hot days. A lovely texture is produced by churning fresh fruit juices or coffee with sugar and water to make granita, a semi-frozen dessert. Granita, which comes in a number of flavors like lemon, almond, and strawberry, pairs well with a soft, buttery brioche bun for the ideal balance of sweet and salty. This typical breakfast or afternoon snack from Sicily is an integral element of Palermo's culinary culture.

Take a Sicilian Culinary Adventure

Traditional Sicilian meals from Palermo provide a window into the rich flavors, cultural influences, and time-honored traditions that have created the city's culinary legacy.

gastronomy. Make sure to go beyond the usual dishes mentioned above as you explore Palermo's culinary scene and learn about additional local specialties.

Try some of the delicious street food options, such panelle (chickpea fritters) and sfincione (pizza made in the style of Sicily). Enjoy delicious prawns, soft octopus, and sweet red mullet as you indulge in the briny taste of fresh seafood. Don't pass up the chance to sample special delicacies like pasta con le sarde, which combines sardines with wild fennel, pine nuts, and other peculiar flavors.

To go along with your gastronomic adventure, visit the nearby vineyards and taste some of Sicily's world-renowned wines. Crisp whites, robust reds, and superb dessert wines like Marsala are among the island's well-known wine offerings.

Explore Palermo's trattorias and osterias for an authentic dining experience, where you can enjoy homestyle Sicilian cuisine made with love and passion. Talk to the welcoming locals; they are always willing to share their favorite foods and culinary customs.

Palermo offers a culinary experience that will make a lasting impression, whether you decide to eat in classy restaurants, sample street cuisine from market stalls, or savor traditional delicacies in family-run institutions. Get ready for a culinary adventure where every taste reveals the enticing flavors, fascinating history, and welcoming atmosphere that characterize Palermo's culinary scene.

Best Palermo Restaurants

Palermo is a treasury of gastronomic pleasures and is known for its bustling food scene and extensive culinary heritage. The city offers a wide variety of culinary alternatives to please even the most discriminating palates, from classic Sicilian delicacies to cutting-edge inventions. Explore the finest restaurants in Palermo as you embark on a gastronomic adventure where the flavors of the Mediterranean come to life and where outstanding cuisine is coupled with gracious hospitality to create an unforgettable dining experience.

Buatta's Restaurant

Ristorante Buatta, which is situated in the center of Palermo, is a gastronomic treasure that expertly combines tradition and modernity. The inventive food at this

Michelin-starred restaurant, which features the finest local ingredients prepared precisely and artistically, mesmerizes diners. Each plate at Ristorante Buatta is a work of art, exquisitely presented and brimming with flavors, ranging from delicate fish dishes to opulent meat creations. Allow the skilled chefs to take you on a memorable culinary adventure while you immerse yourself in the magnificent setting.

San Francesco Antica Focacceria

Visit Antica Focacceria San Francesco, a famous restaurant that has been serving traditional Sicilian food since 1834, to have a taste of Palermo's culinary heritage. With its wonderful vintage decor and cozy atmosphere, this historic restaurant will take you back in time as soon as you enter.

Enjoy traditional dishes made with genuine flavors and ingredients acquired locally, such as arancini, pasta alla Norma, and caponata. A valued institution, Antica Focacceria San Francesco is renowned for its enduring charm and delectable Sicilian delicacies. It is cherished by both locals and tourists alike.

Osteria dei Vespri

Osteria dei Vespri is a culinary sanctuary that embraces the flavors of Sicily in a modern environment. It is tucked away in the center of Palermo's historic area. The menu at this classy restaurant features the region's best seasonal ingredients and age-old recipes for a sophisticated dining experience.

The dishes of Osteria dei Vespri are a symphony of tastes, masterfully prepared to highlight the best of Sicilian cuisine, and range from delectable seafood dishes to flawlessly cooked meats. Allow the attentive staff to lead you on a culinary adventure as you pair your meal with a fine wine from their enormous collection.

Trattoria Biondo

Trattoria Biondo is a must-visit if you want to experience Palermo's culinary heritage firsthand. Since generations past, this family-run trattoria has delighted guests with its robust Sicilian fare. Pasta con le sarde, swordfish rolls, and sicilian cassata for dessert are among the many traditional favorites on the menu. You will have an outstanding eating experience that will make you feel like a member of the family thanks to the welcoming ambiance and genuine hospitality of the Biondo family.

Gagini Restaurant

Ristorante Gagini, located in a historic structure in Palermo, offers a sophisticated dining experience that honors Sicilian cuisine with a modern touch. The dishes on the menu, which was created by acclaimed chef Agostino

Gagini, highlight the best local ingredients. Each plate is a wonderful combination of flavors and textures, from delicate seafood dishes to expertly prepared meat entrees. Enjoy a dining experience that blends history and innovation as you lose yourself in the exquisite setting accented with modern artwork and subdued lighting.

Enjoy Palermo's Delights in Cuisine

The culinary culture in Palermo is vibrant, diversified, and steeped in history, much like the city itself. Palermo provides a variety of eating experiences to suit every taste and budget, from Michelin-starred restaurants to lovely trattorias. The top restaurants in the city are prepared to excite your taste buds and highlight the extraordinary flavors of Sicily, whether you're looking for upscale gourmet cuisine or hearty traditional dishes.

Restaurant A' Cuccagna

When you enter Trattoria A' Cuccagna, you'll be whisked away to a world of deliciously authentic Sicilian cuisine. This family-run trattoria embraces the idea of "farm-to-table," obtaining the finest ingredients from regional suppliers and creating delectable dishes with them. Regional staples including spaghetti with sardines, eggplant parmigiana, and robust stews are highlighted on the menu. A unique eating experience that embodies Sicilian hospitality is produced by the warm and welcoming setting combined with pleasant service.

Merced's Osteria

Osteria Mercede is a hidden gem that thrills foodies with its creative approach to Sicilian cuisine. It is tucked away in a lovely alley in the center of Palermo. Traditional dishes are improved by the skilled cooks at Osteria Mercede by adding innovative touches and cutting-edge methods. Each meal is an exquisite symphony of tastes that has been carefully created and presented. Enjoy saffron risotto, soft braised meats, and superb desserts that exhibit the ideal harmony of sweet and savory flavors.

I Pupi

Visit I Pupi, a restaurant that honors Sicilian puppetry and culinary heritage, for a really unique dining experience. The restaurant's interior is decorated with vibrant puppets and traditional Sicilian artwork, which gives the space a whimsical feel that takes you back in time. Traditional cuisine served with a modern touch are on the menu at I Pupi. Every mouthful reveals the tradition and fervor of Sicilian cuisine, from the fresh seafood to the handcrafted pasta and succulent meat entrees.

Blues, bye-bye

Go to Bye Bye Blues if you're in the mood for Sicilian food with a contemporary twist. This hip restaurant uses fusion cuisine to offer a distinctive and thrilling eating experience by fusing Sicilian ingredients with global influences.

The menu offers dishes that highlight the inventiveness and skill of the cooks, with choices ranging from sushi rolls made in the style of Sicily to shrimp ceviche with citrus fruits. Enjoy the vivid and lively environment of this trendy Palermo restaurant while sipping on a homemade cocktail or a glass of Sicilian wine with your meal.

Take a Deep Dive Into Palermo's Culinary Scene

The top eateries in Palermo are examples of the region's delectable cuisine and the city's thriving food scene. Each eating location offers a different viewpoint on Sicilian cuisine, from traditional trattorias to cutting-edge culinary experiences. So, appreciate the flavors of Palermo, admire the enthusiasm and ingenuity of its cooks, and let the city's culinary culture to take you on an unforgettable culinary adventure.

The top restaurants in Palermo are prepared to delight and satiate your cravings for food, whether you're a food enthusiast, an adventurous eater, or simply looking for an authentic Sicilian dining experience.

Pubs, bars, and cafes

Beyond its celebrated food scene, Palermo has a vibrant and active ambiance that includes a thriving café culture, busy bars, and welcoming pubs. Palermo provides a variety of options for those looking for a delectable drink and a friendly atmosphere, from indulging in innovative cocktails at fashionable bars to enjoying freshly brewed coffee in a historic café. Join the residents as they congregate to mingle, relax, and enjoy the lively nightlife of the city.

Old Coffee Spinnato

Visit Antico Caffè Spinnato, a historic café that has been serving Palermo since 1860, and travel back in time. The café's opulent atmosphere, which is furnished with antiques, gives off an old-world appeal that takes you back in time. Enjoy delicious pastries and classic Sicilian delicacies while sipping on an expertly crafted espresso or indulging in a creamy cappuccino. More than just a coffee shop, Antico Caffè Spinnato is a cultural hub where locals and tourists meet to appreciate the finer points of coffee making and the inviting atmosphere of Palermo.

Garibaldi, Bar

Bar Garibaldi is a well-liked gathering place that has been a local favorite for ages and is situated in the center of Palermo's historic area. This lively café-bar is the perfect location to unwind with a cool Aperol Spritz as the sun sets or to start your day with a robust Sicilian espresso. The outside dining area offers the ideal vantage point for people-watching and getting lost in Palermo's energetic environment. Join the buzzing group, strike up a discussion, and allow Bar Garibaldi's allure to absorb you.

clandestine brewery

At Birrificio Clandestino, a craft brewery and tavern that has become a hotspot for beer aficionados in Palermo, beer fans will find their home. Each of the brewery's handcrafted beers is meticulously produced to provide a one-of-a-kind and outstanding drinking experience. Sit down at the bar and try some of their brews, which range from deep stouts and crisp wheat beers to zesty IPAs. The skilled and affable staff is always willing to share their love of beer and to lead you through the tasting process.

Piazza Dei Papiri

Piazza dei Papiri is a hidden gem that guarantees an outstanding experience for a chic evening of cocktails and ambiance. This stylish bar has a sizable cocktail menu that combines traditional cocktails with contemporary twists. Drink a carefully prepared Negroni or indulge in a specialty cocktail with Sicilian tastes. A refined night of indulgence is made possible by the attractive interior's gentle lighting and chic decor.

Discover Palermo's Exciting Nightlife

- The vibrant and friendly atmosphere of Palermo is reflected in the city's café, bar, and pub scene. Palermo has everything you might want, whether you're looking for the character of a vintage café, the vigor of a busy bar, or the originality of a small brewery. As you go out on a voyage through the energetic nightlife of the city, immerse yourself in the local culture, socialize with welcoming people, and take in the flavors of Palermo. Palermo's cafés, bars, and pubs offer a mixture of flavor and ambiance that will leave you desiring more, whether you choose a strong espresso to start your day or a properly made cocktail to close the night.

Options for entertainment and nightlife

Palermo comes to life after sunset with a thriving nightlife that hums with excitement and activity. Palermo has a wide range of entertainment alternatives to suit every taste, from hip nightclubs and live music venues to cultural events and theater productions. Discover Palermo's exciting nightlife as you immerse yourself in the city's alluring atmosphere.

Playhouse Massimo

The Teatro Massimo is a cultural landmark that exemplifies the splendor of performing arts and is one of the biggest opera houses in Europe. Opera, ballet, and classical music concerts are just a few of the performances that take place in this magnificent theater. Enter the vast theater, which is decorated with exquisite details, and spend the evening being inspired by performances by top-tier performers. The Teatro Massimo is more than just a place to go; it's a journey into the world of culture and the arts.

Zisa's Cantieri Culturali

Cantieri Culturali della Zisa, a bustling cultural center offering a diverse range of art exhibitions, live performances, and music events, is housed in a former industrial complex. Visit the galleries to explore the wide variety of modern art on display there or attend a live music performance by both regional and international musicians. Cantieri Culturali della Zisa is a must-visit for art fans and those interested in getting a taste of Palermo's alternative culture since the industrial attractiveness of the location provides a special atmosphere to the cultural experience.

Palermo's Baroque Palaces and Aristocratic Society

Palermo's magnificent baroque mansions, many of which have been converted into upscale clubs and nightlife establishments, are a testament to the city's rich heritage. These opulent settings provide a magnificent backdrop for a fantastic night out. Dance the night away in lavish ballrooms decorated with elaborate frescoes and crystal chandeliers, or unwind in chic lounges while taking in a specially crafted beverage menu and live music. The baroque palaces of Palermo offer a spectacular and affluent nightlife experience while affording an insight into the city's aristocratic past.

Market in Vucciria at night

Vucciria Market is bustling with bustle during the day as locals and tourists browse the colorful stalls. But as night sets, the market becomes a center for nightlife and delicious street cuisine. Experience the vibrant atmosphere as the market comes to life with live music, street entertainers, and a tantalizing assortment of food vendors serving authentic Sicilian street food. Enjoy freshly grilled fish, panelle, and arancini as you take in the bustling atmosphere of Vucciria Market after dark.

Participate in Palermo's Nighttime Adventures

You are invited to explore Palermo after hours by the city's vibrant nightlife and entertainment scene. Palermo provides a variety of activities to suit every taste, from the splendor of the Teatro Massimo to the alternative cultural hubs and lively street markets.

Whatever your preference, Palermo's nightlife and entertainment alternatives will leave you with priceless memories and a deeper understanding of the city's vibrant energy. Whether you choose a night of high culture, dancing until dawn, or immersing yourself in the city's alternative scene. Prepare to embrace the night and let the colorful energy of Palermo enthrall you.

CHAPTER 5

Shopping in Palermo

In addition to being a city steeped in history and culture, Palermo is a shopping paradise that satisfies the needs of people who enjoy fashion, fine art, and finding one-of-a-kind treasures. Palermo provides a wide variety of shopping experiences that capture the unique character and taste of the city, from luxury boutiques and designer shops to lively markets and artisan crafts. Get ready for a shopping excursion that will leave you with treasured purchases and a greater understanding of Palermo's distinctive shopping environment.

Popular Streets and Markets for Shopping

For those looking for a one-of-a-kind shopping experience, Palermo is a paradise. Here, traditional practices coexist with modern aesthetics to create a dynamic tapestry of markets and shopping lanes. Palermo has a wide variety of shopping alternatives to suit all tastes and budgets, from crowded street markets to elegant boutiques. Explore Palermo's bustling markets and shopping districts to immerse yourself in the city's dynamic shopping scene and find hidden gems.

Via della Libertà

Via della Libertà is the place to go if you want a taste of luxury. High-end fashion boutiques, designer shops, and well-known brands fill this attractive street. Take in the glitzy atmosphere of this luxury shopping area as you stroll along the broad sidewalks lined with palm trees. Via della

Libertà caters to sophisticated shoppers who value the finer things in life, offering everything from top international fashion brands to exquisite jewelry and accessories.

Via Maqueda

The historically significant and charming Via Maqueda provides a blend of antique stores and modern businesses. The lively squares of Quattro Canti and Piazza Pretoria are connected by this busy roadway that goes through the center of Palermo.

Discover the diverse assortment of shops that line Via Maqueda, providing anything from handcrafted goods and unique souvenirs to fashionable clothing and accessories. Don't pass up the chance to sample delectable street fare from the neighborhood vendors as you stroll down this ancient commercial avenue.

Vucciria Market

Experience the energetic ambiance of Vucciria Market, a revered marketplace that was established in the 13th century. With its vibrant kiosks, fragrant spices, and energetic atmosphere, this crowded market is a sensory feast. Discover a variety of goods at the vendors, including fresh fruit, regional cheeses, cured meats, and authentic Sicilian delicacies. Engage in polite conversation with the vendors as you peruse the market and take in the lively energy that distinguishes Palermo's street markets.

Market Ballar

Visit Ballar Market for a genuine and realistic shopping experience. This busy market captures the essence of Palermo. With its vivid displays of fruits, vegetables, seafood, spices, and local goods, this lively market is a feast for the senses.

You can interact with the helpful merchants and practice the skill of haggling as you walk through the small lanes. Ballar Market is more than simply a place to shop; it's also a cultural experience that offers a window into Palermo locals' daily routines and traditions.

Discover Palermo's Hidden Shopping Gems

For all compulsive shoppers and intrepid explorers, Palermo's shopping districts and marketplaces offer a variety and enthralling experience. Palermo has plenty to offer, whether you're looking for upscale brands, unusual mementos, or a taste of regional cuisine.

As you discover hidden treasures and make enduring memories, take in the lively environment, mingle with the amiable locals, and let the city's shopping scene charm you. Palermo cordially invites you to revel in a shopping paradise where vintage fashion meets cutting-edge design.

Local Goods and Memorabilia

Palermo provides a wide variety of regional goods and mementos that perfectly capture the spirit of the city thanks to its rich cultural heritage and lively customs. Palermo offers a treasure trove of genuine goods that let you bring a piece of the city home with you, from handcrafted goods and regional specialties to one-of-a-kind keepsakes and chic souvenirs. Learn about the unique goods and trinkets produced locally that encapsulate Palermo's character and serve as priceless mementos of your visit.

Potteries And Ceramics

Palermo is well known for its magnificent pottery and ceramics, which showcase the city's creative flare and skill. Find exquisitely hand-painted plates, bowls, and vases with elaborate motifs derived from Sicilian customs in the neighborhood shops and workshops. Ceramics make for classy and enduring keepsakes, whether you opt for a bright piece with traditional themes or a modern design that expresses the spirit of Palermo.

Delicacies from Sicily

Bring some of the mouthwatering treats from Sicily back home to indulge in the region's delights. Palermo provides a broad variety of culinary delights, from locally produced olive oil and sun-dried tomatoes to sweet sweets like cannoli and almond pastries. To find top-notch goods that represent the genuine flavors of Sicily, visit specialty food shops and marketplaces. These delectable delicacies make wonderful presents or a tantalizing memento of your visit to Palermo.

Handmade Leather Products

The fine leather goods that can be seen all around the city are a testament to Palermo's long history of leather production. The regional craftspeople expertly produce items that skillfully combine conventional methods with modern designs, from chic handbags and wallets to exquisitely created belts and accessories. Consider purchasing a piece of handcrafted leather as a memento that captures Palermo's flair and workmanship.

Puppets and marionettes

Invest in a classic marionette or puppet to fully immerse yourself in the world of Sicilian puppetry. A centuries-old art form that has a special place in Sicilian culture, these delicately drawn characters are created by talented craftspeople. These charming, colorful masterpieces are one-of-a-kind keepsakes that perfectly embody the spirit of Palermo's traditional entertainment.

Accessories and Clothing with a Palermo motif

Wear and accessorize with a touch of Palermo's charm everywhere you go by drawing inspiration from the city's recognizable emblems and monuments. Look for fashionable t-shirts, totes, or hats with illustrations of Palermo's architectural marvels, including the Palermo Cathedral or the Teatro Massimo. These stylish accessories are conversation openers as well as serving as a memento of your time spent in Palermo.

Accept Palermo's Genuine Treasures

Local wares and mementos from Palermo provide a look into the city's extensive cultural history and artistic traditions. Each item conveys a story and provides a concrete link to the colorful atmosphere of Palermo, whether you choose to purchase exquisitely created pottery, delicious treats, or artisanal leather products. Accept these genuine treasures, assist neighborhood craftspeople, and allow Palermo's spirit to stay with you long after your trip to this alluring city.

Designer and boutique stores

The city of Palermo, which is renowned for its perfect sense of style and fashion, has a thriving assortment of boutique boutiques and designer outlets that appeal to discerning customers looking for distinctive and premium clothing. Palermo's fashion culture is a hidden gem just waiting to be discovered, with everything from premium boutiques presenting well-known Italian designers to hip concept stores promoting up-and-coming local talent.

Discover the boutique businesses and designer outlets that make up Palermo's fashion scene to enter the world of glitz and elegance.

Via della Libertà

With its classy, tree-lined avenue, Via della Libertà is home to a wide variety of posh boutiques and designer shops that ooze refinement and luxury. This elegant boulevard features well-known Italian and worldwide fashion labels, giving discerning customers the chance to splurge on high-end clothing. Explore the collections of renowned designers as you look for the ideal statement piece to add to your wardrobe and immerse yourself in a world of couture and chic elegance.

Via Ruggero Settimo

Via Ruggero Settimo, a chic boulevard in the center of Palermo, is dotted with a mix of premium boutiques and cutting-edge designer shops. Fashion-conscious people looking for chic clothing and accessories are drawn to this busy retail area.

Discover the expertly chosen boutiques displaying both well-known designers and up-and-coming local artists. For those looking for a dash of elegance with a contemporary twist, Via Ruggero Settimo provides an alluring selection of fashion-forward items, including stylish clothing and distinctive accessories.

Multibrand Boutiques and Concept Stores

A number of concept stores and multibrand boutiques that feature a carefully curated assortment of up-and-coming designers and distinctive fashion labels are also part of

Palermo's fashion scene. These chic locations give independent designers a stage on which to display their originality and skill. Discover one-of-a-kind clothing, accessories, and lifestyle items that capture Palermo's fashion-forward vibe by entering these cutting-edge locations decorated with modern aesthetics.

Retro & Vintage Finds

Contemporary styles are just one aspect of Palermo's fashion scene. The city also has a variety of retro and vintage shops that appeal to people looking for one-of-a-kind, sentimental items. Join us on a treasure hunt around Palermo's picturesque alleyways and discover hidden treasures filled with retro apparel, accessories, and jewelry that embody the spirit of bygone times. As you browse these magical shops, uncover a piece of fashion history and appreciate the attraction of antique clothing.

Experience Palermo's Excellence in Fashion
You are invited to go on a fashion adventure where style, elegance, and creativity combine at Palermo's boutique shops and designer boutiques. Palermo has a fashion scene

that will satisfy even the most discerning shopper, whether they are looking for high-end couture, cutting-edge designs, or vintage finds. Discover one-of-a-kind items made by skilled designers, bask in the chic atmosphere of the city, and elevate your sense of style with Palermo's boutique boutiques and designer outlets.

CHAPTER 6

Day Trips from Palermo

While Palermo is a fascinating city with a wide variety of sights to see and things to do, traveling outside of its boundaries reveals a world of undiscovered natural beauty, historic monuments, and little communities. Explore the various landscapes and cultural riches that surround this dynamic city by setting off on a day excursion from Palermo. These day tours give a chance to explore deeper into Sicily's rich past and magnificent beauty, visiting anything from ancient ruins to lovely seaside towns.

Monreale

The town of Monreale, which is only a short drive from Palermo, entices visitors with its magnificent architecture and extensive cultural legacy. An unforgettable day trip to Monreale reveals a remarkable fusion of culture, the arts, and beautiful scenery. Monreale is famed for its magnificent Cathedral, a true masterpiece of Norman architecture and a symbol of Sicilian beauty. It is perched on a slope overlooking the scenic Conca d'Oro (Golden Shell) valley.

The Monreale Cathedral

- The magnificent Cathedral, a symbol of the island's rich cultural past, should be the focal point of any trip to Monreale. Step inside to enter a world of stunning architecture and creative brilliance. Over 6,500 square meters of golden mosaics that represent biblical events and highlight the craftsmanship of Byzantine craftsmen adorn the interior. Admire the mosaics' minute intricacies, vibrant colors, and the tasteful blending of Byzantine, Arab, and Norman elements that characterize the Cathedral's distinct design.

The Benedictines' Cloister

- The Benedictine Cloister is a peaceful haven next to the Cathedral that radiates peace and elegance. Take a leisurely stroll through the cloister's tastefully built space, which is embellished with delicately carved columns and attractive arches. The tranquil sanctuary provided by the center garden, which is surrounded by luxuriant foliage and enticing flowers, allows you to pause and consider Monreale's creative and spiritual legacy.

Exploring the Town and sweeping Views

- While Monreale's Cathedral is unquestionably its most notable feature, the town itself has many attractions to discover. Enjoy a leisurely stroll through the quaint alleyways adorned with classic Sicilian homes and take in the genuine atmosphere of this old town. Visit the tiny stores that provide regional handicrafts and goods as you stroll for a chance to take some of Monreale's charm home with you.

The Conca d'Oro valley, Palermo, and the glistening Tyrrhenian Sea beyond can all be seen in great detail from the Belvedere Square, where you can also get panoramic views. This vantage point provides a stunning viewpoint that perfectly captures the allure of the area.

Enjoying Sicilian food

- A trip to Monreale wouldn't be complete without experiencing Sicilian cuisine's delights. Enjoy some of the regional specialties at one of the quaint trattorias or cafés dotted about the town. Arancini (fried rice balls), pasta alla Norma (pasta with eggplant and ricotta salata cheese), and cannoli (crisp pastry filled with sweet ricotta cream) are a few examples of classic Sicilian cuisine. Drink some local wine with your lunch, and let Sicily's flavors whisk you away to gastronomic paradise.

Monreale, A Timeless Beauty

A visit to Monreale for the day is a journey through architectural beauty and cultural diversity. The town's treasures will enthrall and inspire you, from the majestic Cathedral to the serene cloister. Discover the picturesque alleyways of Monreale, take in the beauty of its mosaics, and experience the flavors of Sicilian food. Discover the timeless beauty of Monreale, a place close to Palermo where history and art combine to produce a memorable experience.

Cefalù

The picturesque coastal town of Cefalù is not far from Palermo and entices visitors with its allure, natural beauty, and lengthy past. A day excursion to Cefalù is the ideal way to get away from the busy city and experience the peacefulness of the Mediterranean while also discovering historical sites and enjoying the luxuries of seaside living.

The Old City and the Dome

- Start your day excursion by seeing Cefalù's historic core, which is the city's beating heart. Spend some time getting lost in the maze of winding cobblestone lanes that are lined with vibrant homes, adorable shops, and warm cafés. Find out-of-the-way squares with quaint fountains and bustling piazzas where locals and tourists congregate. The beautiful Duomo, a UNESCO World Heritage Site, is at the epicenter of it all. Admire its commanding exterior and the ornate mosaics that cover the inside, which represent biblical scenes with breathtaking workmanship. For sweeping views of the town and the glistening Mediterranean Sea, climb to the rooftop deck.

La Rocca and the Beach

- Without taking a leisurely stroll along the city's lovely beach, no trip to Cefalù is complete. Put your feet in the fine, golden sand, let the cool sea wind caress your skin, and listen to the waves' hypnotic beat. Swim in the cool, crystal-clear water, or just relax in the warmth of the sun.

A hike to La Rocca is available for those who are more daring. This majestic rock towers above the town and provides breath-taking panoramas of the nearby countryside and the coast. Set out on the path that ascends the steep hills while passing historic sites and stunning natural scenery. Reach the top, and you'll be rewarded with breath-taking views and a sense of accomplishment.

Local Food & Gastronomic Delights

- Take advantage of Cefalù's culinary offerings after a morning of exploring. Treat your taste buds to the delights of Sicilian cuisine by looking for a quaint trattoria or seafood restaurant. Enjoy dishes made with fresh seafood like grilled fish, sarde a beccafico (stuffed sardines), or spaghetti ai frutti di mare (pasta with mixed seafood). Enjoy the harmonious fusion of tastes that represent the region's culinary tradition by serving your meal with a glass of Sicilian wine.

Craft stores and souvenir shopping

- Take the time to peruse the artisan stores that feature regional workmanship as you stroll through Cefalù's streets. Discover one-of-a-kind jewelry, handwoven fabrics, and ceramics that showcase the ingenuity and craftsmanship of Sicilian craftspeople. These items make wonderful keepsakes that let you bring a bit of Cefalù's charm and craftsmanship home.

A coastal gem is Cefalù

- An lovely getaway into a beach paradise is what a day trip to Cefalù offers. Enjoy the delicacies of

Sicilian cuisine while you soak up the history of its historic streets and sunbathe on its magnificent beach. Allow Cefalù's splendor to seize your attention and leave you with priceless memories of this seaside treasure.

Segesta

- Take a day excursion to Segesta, a fascinating archaeological site tucked away in the picturesque countryside of western Sicily, to escape the bustle of Palermo. This historic city gives a trip back in time and the chance to fully appreciate Sicily's rich history and natural beauty thanks to its well-preserved Greek remains and gorgeous surroundings.

Greece's Temple

- The stately Greek temple in Segesta is the town's finest achievement. It is a magnificent example of Doric architecture and is perched on a hill amid olive trees and rolling green slopes. Admire the temple's magnificence and the slender columns' ageless elegance that have remained in place throughout the years. Allow your imagination to take you back in time as you take a leisurely stroll through the site.

The Theater

- The ancient theater of Segesta, a unique building carved into the hillside, is located next to the temple. Imagine the shows and spectacles that once provided entertainment for the locals of this old city as you climb the stairs and take a seat. Enjoy sweeping views of the surroundings, including the glittering Gulf of Castellammare, from the theater's vantage point.

Stunning Countryside

Segesta offers stunning panoramas of the Sicilian countryside in addition to the ancient site. Take a leisurely stroll over the undulating hills' quiet pathways, which are strewn with wildflowers and fragrant plants. Take a deep breath and enjoy nature's tranquility. Make careful to capture the wonder of Segesta in your photographs because the scenery's magnificence offers many options for photography.

The town called Calatafimi

Explore the surrounding town of Calatafimi to round off your day excursion. This quaint Sicilian village, perched on a hilltop, provides a window into everyday life and the chance to sample regional cuisine in its original form. Take in the laid-back ambiance as you stroll along the winding lanes packed with classic homes and artisan businesses. Enjoy a leisurely lunch at one of the neighborhood trattorias, where you can sample dishes created in the classic Sicilian style using fresh, regional ingredients.

Segesta is a historic settlement

An excursion to Segesta is a trip back in time and a chance to interact with ancient cultures. Enjoy the majesty of the Greek temple, wonder at the historic theater, and take in the tranquility of the nearby countryside. Experience the local cuisine and culture by traveling to the nearby town of Calatafimi. Discover the traces of the past, and let Segesta's fascinating history inspire your creativity. This day tour promises to be an unforgettable excursion that will give you a newfound respect for Sicily's priceless antiquities.

Erice

The charming hilltop hamlet of Erice is only a short drive from Palermo and offers a pleasant day excursion that takes you back in time. Erice promises a fascinating journey through history and the ability to fully immerse yourself in this mountain sanctuary's tranquillity with its medieval beauty, historic walls, and beautiful vistas.

The Venus Castle

- The Castle of Venus, which is majestically placed on the town's highest point, is a must-see on any trip to Erice. A sensation of amazement overtakes you as you ascend the twisting streets and pass through the old gates. On a clear day, explore the castle's ruins, historic walls, and watchtowers, which provide expansive views over the region's landscape, coastline, and even the distant Egadi Islands. Learn about the tales and legends surrounding this legendary location, and allow your imagination to take you back in time.

Medieval Architecture and Streets

- Walking through Erice's winding, cobblestone streets is like entering a medieval fairytale. Admire the stone homes, arched doors, and elaborate balconies of the well-preserved architecture. Discover the quaint cafes and fountain-adorned tiny squares, where you may unwind and take in the tranquil atmosphere of the town. Allow yourself to become lost in the maze-like lanes so you can discover hidden treasures like charming artisan studios and specialty shops selling regional specialties.

Churches and historic sites

- Historic sites and churches may be found all across Erice as a testament to its illustrious past. Visit the spectacular Duomo, which is devoted to the Assumption of the Virgin Mary, and be in awe of the gorgeous artwork and intricate architectural elements. Enter the beautiful paintings that depict biblical scenes with skillful brushstrokes in the Church of San Giovanni. Consider taking a few moments to light a candle and meditate in the peaceful environment of these holy places.

Pastry treats and gastronomic pleasures

- Without indulging in some of the town's famous pastries, a trip to Erice would not be complete.

Enjoy the local delicacy "genovesi," delectable pastries stuffed with creamy custard or ricotta cream. Let your senses be enticed by the flavors of your delight and a cup of fragrant Sicilian coffee. In one of the quaint trattorias, you may indulge in meals prepared using regional products and time-honored techniques for a heartier supper that features classic Sicilian cuisine.

A Timeless Retreat: Erice

- A day excursion to Erice provides a window into a quiet and charming medieval environment. Discover the castle, stroll through the medieval streets, and take in the atmosphere of the past. Explore obscure nooks and take in the beauty of the churches and sites. Enjoy the sweet treats of the town and the flavors of Sicilian food. Make memories that will last long beyond your visit to this mountain refuge by letting Erice immerse you in its timeless embrace.

Agrigento

Explore Agrigento, a UNESCO World Heritage Site famed for its historic ruins and abundant archaeological discoveries, on an exciting day excursion from Palermo. Agrigento, which is situated on the southern coast of Sicily, gives you a wonderful look at the magnificence of the ancient world and lets you immerse yourself in the intriguing history of this remarkable city.

The Temples' Valley

- The Valley of the Temples, a sizable archaeological site that houses some of the best-preserved Greek temples outside of Greece, is the centerpiece of any trip to Agrigento. Enjoy a leisurely stroll through the park as you take in the magnificence of these historic buildings. Imagine the events and rituals that were performed inside the magnificent Temple of Concordia as you admire its wonderfully preserved columns and detailed embellishments. Discover the Hera-dedicated Temple of Juno, and as you stand in awe of its architectural magnificence, feel the weight of history. The ruins of additional temples, such the Temple of Hercules and the Temple of Castor and Pollux, become apparent as you stroll through this historic environment; each has an own tale to tell.

The Museum of Archaeology

- Visit the neighboring Archaeological Museum of Agrigento after exploring the Valley of the Temples. Here, you can learn more about the historic city's history and culture. Admire the large collection of relics, which sheds light on the daily activities and artistic accomplishments of the people who formerly lived in this area. These artifacts include statues, pottery, and elaborate gold jewelry. Your awareness and enjoyment of Agrigento's extensive historical legacy are further enhanced by the museum's exhibitions.

The Cathedral and Old Town

- Enjoy a leisurely stroll around the old town of Agrigento, where Baroque and medieval elements harmoniously coexist. Admire the Cathedral of San

Gerlando's magnificent interior and elaborate exterior as you take in its stunning architecture. Discover the charming boutiques, cozy cafes, and tiny lanes surrounded by old buildings where you can sample authentic Sicilian cuisine and take in the lively atmosphere of the city.

Scale of the Turks

- Agrigento's Scala dei Turchi, a magnificent white rock structure that looks out over the Mediterranean Sea's turquoise seas, is a special natural wonder worth visiting. Admire the tiered limestone cliffs that resemble a majestic staircase that have been carved by wind and water over time. Enjoy the sun while taking a leisurely stroll down the beach and taking in the expansive views of the coastline. Before returning to Palermo, the Scala dei Turchi offers a peaceful haven that is the ideal spot to relax.

A Journey into Antiquity in Agrigento

- An remarkable voyage into the ancient world is promised by a day trip to Agrigento. Discover relics at the Archaeological Museum, stroll through the streets of the ancient town, and explore the magnificent temples in the Valley of the Temples. Enjoy the delights of Sicilian food while taking in this wonderful city's ageless beauty. Agrigento provides a day of exploration and discovery that will leave you with long-lasting recollections of Sicily's rich history, from the grandeur of the past to the stunning natural scenery.

CHAPTER 7

Outdoor Activities and Recreation

In addition to having a wealth of historical and cultural sites, Palermo, the lively capital of Sicily, also provides a wide range of outdoor sports and recreational options for outdoor enthusiasts and adventure seekers. Palermo's natural playground invites you to set out on exhilarating experiences and immerse yourself in the splendor of nature, from spectacular coastal views to lush mountains and lovely countryside.

Exploration of the Coast

Palermo's breathtaking coastline entices you to go seaside exploring. Enjoy a leisurely stroll along the sandy beaches as you listen to the lapping of the warm Mediterranean waters. Enjoy the warmth of the sun, unwind on a beach towel, and take in the tranquility of the ocean. Take part in water sports like swimming, snorkeling, or paddleboarding for more strenuous activities. Investigate hidden caverns and coves to learn about the mysteries of the aquatic world. Palermo's coastline offers a variety of scenery to delight every outdoor enthusiast, from sandy beaches to jagged cliffs.

Picnics and outdoor excursions
Retreat to the serene parks and nature reserves that dot Palermo's terrain to get away from the city's noise and bustle. Find a shady location under a tree, fill a picnic basket with regional specialties, and unwind in the serene atmosphere of the surroundings. The parks in Palermo are a refuge of greenery where you can unwind, read a book, or just spend time with friends and family.

Enjoy the wildflower scents and the sounds of birds as you stroll gently along the nature pathways. Palermo's nature retreats offer a tranquil haven and an opportunity to unwind amidst the splendor of the surrounding landscape.

For both nature lovers and adventure seekers, Palermo offers a variety of outdoor pursuits and leisure possibilities. Palermo's natural playground allows you to engage in thrilling outdoor activities, such as coastal exploration, hiking expeditions, bicycle misadventures, and peaceful picnics. As you immerse yourself in the great outdoors, embrace the beauty of nature, uncover hidden gems, and make priceless memories. Palermo provides a wealth of options to take in the best of Sicily's natural attractions, whether you're looking for peace or excitement.

Palermo beaches

Palermo, has a magnificent shoreline that spans along the Mediterranean Sea's pristine seas. Palermo is a lovely refuge for beach lovers looking for relaxation, sun-soaked activities, and the calming sounds of the waves with its inviting beaches and picturesque coastal scenery. Palermo features a range of coastal havens to suit any inclination, whether you're searching for a kid-friendly beach, a quiet cove, or a lively beachside ambiance.

Beach at Mondello: A Coastal Paradise

Mondello Beach, which is tucked away not far from the city center, is a genuine jewel of Palermo. Visitors come from near and far to this lovely beach because of its fine golden sand and vivid turquoise waves. Families with little children will love the shallow, quiet seas where they may splash and play in the gentle waves. Rentable sun loungers and umbrellas make your beach day comfortable and convenient.

Enjoy the delectable flavors of Sicilian food while taking in the expansive views of the beach by taking a leisurely stroll along the promenade, which is dotted with attractive cafes and restaurants. The natural beauty and lively ambiance of Mondello Beach are the ideal combination.

A Calm Escape at Addaura Beach

Addaura Beach is a great option for those seeking a more quiet and serene beach experience. This hidden gem, which can be found on Palermo's outskirts, provides a tranquil haven away from the city. The beach is tucked away between steep cliffs, giving the area a lovely and exclusive feel. You can relax on the pebbly coast, take in the sunshine, and savor the peace and quiet of the area here. You can explore the abundant marine life that lives below the surface while swimming and snorkeling in the crystal-clear seas. People looking for peace and quiet should head to Addaura Beach.

Isola delle Femmine

Isola delle Femmine is a tiny island just west of Palermo that is home to a clean beach and stunning natural beauty. This picturesque location, which is connected to the mainland by a small isthmus, offers a sense of isolation and tranquillity. A tropical-like atmosphere is created by the sandy beach and clear waters, luring people to enjoy the sunshine and cool sea dips.

The island's attraction is increased by the lush foliage and rugged cliffs that serve as a picturesque backdrop. You can truly get away from the city on Isola delle Femmine, where you can reconnect with the outdoors and experience a tranquil beach setting.

Sun, fun, and water sports at Capaci Beach

Capaci Beach is the ideal beach for people looking for a lively atmosphere and a variety of water sports. This well-known beach resort, which located west of Palermo, offers a lively beachside scene along with a variety of conveniences and recreational opportunities. Sunbathe on the loungers, go parasailing for an exhilarating experience, or learn to windsurf or paddleboard.

In the summer, Capaci Beach is popular for its vibrant atmosphere and busy beach bars where visitors may enjoy cool beverages, live music, and late-night dancing. It's a beach where you may unwind while also feeling a little energized.

Palermo's Beaches: Coastal Bliss

The beaches of Palermo are an invitation to savor the sultry delights of Sicily's coastal splendor. Palermo boasts beaches to suit all tastes, whether you prefer the lively environment of Capaci Beach, the natural paradise of Isola delle Femmine, the quiet seclusion of Addaura Beach, or the family-friendly vibe of Mondello Beach.

Enjoy the beaches of Palermo while soaking in the sun, cooling down in the cool waves, and embracing the easygoing Mediterranean way of life. In addition to providing sun, sand, and tranquility, these coastal retreats provide you the chance to get to know the locals and take part in the colorful beach culture that is so central to Sicilian life.

Remember to bring your beach essentials like sunscreen, a beach towel, and a cap to protect yourself from the sun's rays as you travel to Palermo's beaches. Most beaches include amenities like showers, bathrooms, and beach bars where you may sample delectable regional delicacies and relieve your thirst.

The beaches come alive with a variety of activities and festivals during the summer, giving guests a lively atmosphere. There's usually something going on along

Palermo's shores, from beach volleyball competitions to live music shows. It's a wonderful chance to meet people from the community, make new friends, and become fully immersed in the vibrant beach culture.

Keep the beaches clean and dispose of your rubbish correctly when you visit the beaches to show respect for the environment. Observe any safety precautions or flags that may be present that indicate the state of the water. Always swim in appropriate locations and pay attention to any lifeguard directions.

The beaches of Palermo have something to offer everyone, whether they are looking for relaxation, adventure in the water, or a lively beach scene. These seaside sanctuaries offer a respite from the city and an opportunity to take in the beauty of the Mediterranean coastline, from the kid-friendly sands of Mondello Beach to the quiet seclusion of Addaura Beach. Take advantage of the coastal bliss of Palermo's beaches by gathering your beach gear, soaking in the Sicilian sun, and letting the rhythmic sound of the waves wash away your problems.

Trails For Hiking And Nature

Palermo's varied terrain, which includes mountains, forests, and picturesque countryside, entices travelers to explore its hiking routes and nature trails, unveiling the region's undiscovered natural riches.

The Iconic Mountain that is Monte Pellegrino

The beautiful Monte Pellegrino, which towers majestically above Palermo, is a well-known mountain that provides breath-taking trekking options. Put on your hiking boots and start the ascent to the summit, where you will be rewarded with sweeping views over the city and the glistening Mediterranean Sea.

The paths meander through luxuriant Mediterranean flora that includes fragrant plants, wild flowers, and old trees. As you climb, the air gets crisper and the sounds of nature surround you, giving you a sense of tranquility and an escape from the hustle and bustle of the city. For hikers looking for both breathtaking scenery and unspoiled natural beauty, Monte Pellegrino is a must-see.

The coastal beauty of Zingaro Nature Reserve

The Zingaro Nature Reserve, which is situated on Sicily's northwest coast, is a wonderful treasure for those who love the outdoors. With its rocky cliffs, turquoise bays, and immaculate beaches, this protected area is home to a variety of hiking and nature routes. Explore the rocky shorelines, hidden caverns, and spectacular vistas of the azure sea as you meander along the coastal walks. The reserve is home to a wide variety of plants and animals, including uncommon birds, reptiles, and orchids. Take your time to enjoy the serenity of this unspoiled natural refuge and to fully appreciate its coastline beauty.

Madonie Regional Natural Park

The Madonie Regional Natural Park is the perfect location if you're looking for a mountain hideaway close to Palermo. A huge network of hiking paths wind through gorgeous valleys, historic woods, and quaint mountain towns in this vast park. Immerse yourself in the stark beauty of the surroundings as craggy peaks soar majestically over undulating hills.

Discover unusual flora and animals, including endemic species that are exclusive to this area. A fascinating look into Sicily's past is offered by the park's historical and cultural features, which include old ruins and castles from the Middle Ages. A trip to the Madonie Regional Natural Park guarantees a life-changing trekking adventure through unspoiled environment.

Orleans Nature Trail: Charming Countryside
The Orleans Nature Trail is a secret treasure waiting to be discovered if you explore the area around Palermo's countryside. This picturesque walk offers a view of Sicilian rural life as it meanders through lovely countryside, vineyards, and olive groves. Enjoy the splendor of the rolling hills and pastoral vistas as you stroll along the trail while inhaling the crisp rural air.

Discover historic farms, charming communities, and hospitable people who will make your journey more enjoyable. You may get away from the city and spend some time in the serene Sicilian countryside by taking the Orleans Nature Trail.

Palermo's Natural Escape: Hiking & Nature Trails

A access to Sicily's natural wonders is provided by the hiking and nature paths in Palermo. Palermo has a wide range of outdoor adventure opportunities, including the legendary Monte Pellegrino, the Zingaro Nature Reserve's maritime splendor, the Madonie Regional Natural Park's mountain retreat, and the Orleans Nature Trail's rural allure.

Each route reveals a different aspect of Sicily's natural beauty, showing breath-taking panoramas, varied ecosystems, and a sense of peace that comes from being outside. Grab your hiking supplies, connect with nature, and start exploring Palermo's hiking and nature trails.

It's important to be prepared when hiking these paths. Bring a bag filled with necessities like water, snacks, a map or guidebook, sunscreen, and bug repellent. Wear sturdy hiking shoes and comfortable clothing. For your safety, it's also a good idea to let someone know that you want to go hiking and to stay on the approved trails.

Take the time to become fully immersed in nature as you walk the hiking trails in Palermo. Birdsong, wildflower smells, and geological wonders that have sculpted the environment over time are all enjoyable companions. You can come across secret waterfalls, historic sites, and unusual geological formations along the road, which adds to the attractiveness of these outdoor experiences.

It's important to hike responsibly while exploring these natural places. Respect the environment by adhering to all park rules, keeping on designated trails, and not littering. Take care to protect the wildlife and plants that call these pathways home and leave them in a beautiful state for future generations to enjoy.

The hiking and nature trails in Palermo are suitable for people of all fitness levels and interests, whether they are expert hikers searching for a strenuous ascent or leisurely walkers hoping to connect with nature. Each route has its own unique appeal and benefits, giving you the chance to get away from the city and take in Sicily's wild nature.

Enter the hiking and nature trails of Palermo by lacing up your hiking boots, packing your sense of adventure, and starting off on your excursion. Discover the exhilaration of scaling mountains, relish the serenity of coastal vistas, and taste the charm of the countryside that awaits just outside the city boundaries. You are welcome to explore Palermo's outdoor treasures, which provide a restorative respite and a chance to develop a closer relationship with nature.

Boating and water sports

Palermo, which is tucked away on the Mediterranean Sea's azure coastline, welcomes guests to partake in a variety of thrilling water sports and boating activities. Palermo provides an excellent playground for aquatic activities and unforgettable encounters on the open sea thanks to its crystal-clear waters, pleasant climate, and coastal beauty.

Yachting and Sailing: A Luxury Experience

Set sail for a luxurious and liberating cruise along Palermo's breathtaking coastline. Hire a yacht or sailboat and set out on a relaxing journey filled with discovery and stunning scenery. As you float through the calm waters, you can feel the wind in your hair while taking in the stunning vistas and well-known sites. The marinas in Palermo offer a variety of possibilities to suit your preferences, enabling you to create a unique marine trip whether you are an expert sailor or a novice yachtsman.

Water skiing and jet skiing are fast and exciting sports
Palermo offers the thrills of water skiing and jet skiing for adrenaline seekers who enjoy participating in water sports. As you zip across the waves, driven by the force of the watercraft beneath you, experience the thrill of excitement. Navigate the water while testing your abilities and agility to find the ideal balance between speed and control. Whether you're a novice or seasoned rider, Palermo's coastline offers plenty of room to take part in these adrenaline-pumping water activities and make lifelong memories.

Snorkeling and Scuba Diving: Explore the Underwater World
A fascinating underwater world is waiting to be discovered in the clear seas around Palermo. Immerse yourself in the

fascinating marine ecology by plunging below the surface and going snorkeling or scuba diving. Explore strange tunnels and shipwrecks, see the incredible biodiversity that flourishes beneath the seas, and find vibrant coral reefs teeming with tropical species. Even novices can enjoy the delights of the underwater world in a safe and supervised setting thanks to the availability of certified diving facilities and qualified instructors.

Stand-Up Paddleboarding and Kayaking: Seaside Peace
Kayaking and stand-up paddleboarding are great ways to get away from the throng and have a peaceful experience on the water. Float around Palermo's shoreline while you take in the peace and beauty of the area. Explore isolated beaches, hidden coves, and breathtaking coastal scenery while paddling at your own speed. Enjoy the freedom to explore shallow waters, get up close to the marine life, and take in the serenity that comes with these private water sports.

Discover the Coastline with Boat Tours & Excursions

Consider taking a boat tour or excursion to explore the beauty and charm of Palermo's coastline. Admire the magnificent cliffs, sandy beaches, and untamed rock formations as you cruise along the coastline. Discover undiscovered sea caves, take a dip in remote bays, and take pictures of the coastline fit for a postcard. These trips provide a distinctive viewpoint on Palermo's coastal attractions, whether you opt for a leisurely sightseeing cruise or an action-packed speedboat tour.

Boating and water sports: Explore Palermo's Aquatic Playground

Every water sports fan can find an activity they enjoy in Palermo because to the city's abundance of boating and watersports alternatives. Palermo offers a wide variety of aquatic adventures to sate your thirst, whether you're looking for the luxury of sailing, the rush of jet skiing, the serenity of kayaking, or the wonder of exploring undersea realms.

Put on your wetsuit, gather your equipment, and enter Palermo's aquatic playground. Whether you're an experienced water sports enthusiast or an inquisitive newcomer, Palermo's stunning coastline provides a world of adventure and thrill.

When engaging in water activities, safety comes first, so it's crucial to follow all local laws and regulations. Make sure you have the requisite abilities and expertise before beginning any activity, or think about getting classes from qualified teachers. To ensure a fun and safe trip, familiarize yourself with the sea conditions, tides, and currents.

Palermo's waters offer opportunity for calm exploration and relaxation in addition to the heart-pounding water activities. With a paddleboard that you may rent, you can effortlessly float over the calm seas while taking in the beautiful coastline scenery and the serenity of the ocean. Alternatively, get in a kayak and paddle down the shore to find secluded coves and take in the tranquility of the natural world.

If you would want to go boating and leisurely sight-seeing at the same time, think about signing up for a boat trip or renting a private watercraft. Take a leisurely sail along the coast while taking in the stunning scenery and soaking up the sun. Be amazed by the dramatic cliffs, golden beaches, and charming coastal villages that dot the scenery. Some boat tours even include swimming and snorkeling stops so you can cool off and learn more about the marine life.

Scuba diving is a great option for people looking to have a stronger connection with the aquatic environment. Explore the world of brilliant coral reefs, alive aquatic life, and fascinating shipwrecks by diving beneath the surface. Numerous diving shops in Palermo provide certificates, instruction, and escorted dives for divers of various experience levels. Make lifelong memories by submerging yourself in the aquatic delights.

Keep in mind to respect the marine environment when participating in boating and water sports. Avoid disturbing or harming coral reefs or marine life, and don't trash. Contribute to keeping Palermo's waters beautiful for future generations to enjoy.

Palermo's water activities and boating alternatives may satisfy all tastes, whether you're looking for an exhilarating rush, a tranquil paddle, or a leisurely boat ride. The city's breathtaking shoreline and clear waterways provide the ideal setting for aquatic adventures and life-changing encounters. Therefore, gather your supplies, enjoy the sea wind, and go out on an exciting adventure across Palermo's water wonderland. You are awaiting the delights of the Mediterranean!

CHAPTER 8

Accommodation

Palermo provides a wide variety of lodging choices to satisfy the requirements and tastes of any guest. For travelers looking for a special place to stay, the city offers everything from opulent hotels to welcoming guesthouses.

Opulent Hotel

Palermo is home to a number of opulent hotels that offer visitors an unforgettable stay filled with elegance, extravagance, and unmatched service. These five-star resorts provide an oasis of elegance and tranquillity for the discerning tourist, whether they are tucked away in the city's ancient districts or along its breathtaking coastline.

A historical treasure: Grand Hotel Villa Igiea.
In Palermo, the Grand Hotel Villa Igiea is unquestionably a symbol of luxury. This exquisite hotel, housed in a painstakingly restored Art Nouveau villa, exudes a timeless elegance. The hotel's lovely setting with a view of the Gulf

of Palermo and lush gardens offers spectacular views of the sparkling water. Enter a world of sophisticated rooms that are filled with opulent furnishings and sophisticated touches. Enjoy the roomy suites, each of which has been specially created to offer the greatest in comfort and style.

Enjoy the luxurious amenities offered by the hotel, which include a restorative spa, a private marina, and an elegant restaurant serving excellent Sicilian cuisine. The Grand Hotel Villa Igiea embodies luxury and guarantees a delightful stay in a magnificent environment.

A Combination of History and Modernity at Palazzo Brunaccini

The Palazzo Brunaccini offers a magnificent getaway that combines historical grandeur with cutting-edge design. It is located in the midst of Palermo's historic district. This boutique hotel is housed in a painstakingly renovated 18th-century palace and features a seamless combination of Sicilian architecture and contemporary conveniences.

Admire the ancient furniture, elaborate ceilings, and wonderfully conserved frescoes that grace the lovely interiors. Each room and suite is a haven of comfort, with chic furnishings, luxurious bedding, and cutting-edge conveniences. Enjoy the hotel's rooftop terrace, which provides sweeping views of the metropolitan skyline and a peaceful setting to unwind. The Palazzo Brunaccini provides a haven of contemporary luxury while capturing the sense of Palermo's rich past.

Timeless elegance at the Grand Hotel Wagner

The Grand Hotel Wagner, a famous landmark in Palermo, radiates class and sophistication through the ages. This distinguished hotel, which is situated in the bustling city's commercial centre, provides a haven of elegant elegance. Enter a world of traditional charm where the interiors have been painstakingly created to feature elaborate moldings, glittering chandeliers, and luxurious furnishings.

With modern conveniences and a tasteful fusion of traditional and contemporary decor, the hotel's roomy suites and rooms offer a haven of comfort and tranquility.

Enjoy great meals in the hotel's gourmet restaurant, where Sicilian cuisine takes center stage. The Grand Hotel Wagner is the perfect option for visitors looking for a luxurious stay in Palermo because of its first-rate service, careful attention to detail, and convenient location.

Elegant Retreats: A Memorable Experience

The opulent hotels in Palermo provide a haven of elegance, luxury, and exquisite service, guaranteeing an unforgettable stay in this intriguing city. These lodgings offer an amazing setting to immerse yourself in Palermo's rich culture, bustling ambiance, and stunning beauty, whether you want to live in a historic mansion, a boutique jewel, or a modern paradise. As you set off on a voyage of opulent indulgence in the heart of Palermo, get ready to be pampered, indulged in, and enthralled.

Bed And breakfasts

The vivacious city provides a beautiful selection of bed and breakfasts that capture the friendliness of Sicilian hospitality and give visitors an intimate and genuine experience. These lovely lodgings, which are tucked away in picturesque corners or nestled inside the city's ancient neighborhoods, invite visitors to immerse themselves in the local culture while taking advantage of attentive service and a homey atmosphere.

A Hidden Gem: La Dimora del Genio

La Dimora del Genio is a jewel hidden in the ancient center of Palermo that perfectly encapsulates the beauty of Sicily. The elegantly refurbished 18th-century structure that houses this upscale bed & breakfast has authentic architectural characteristics and nicely designed rooms. Each guest room is deliberately designed, fusing classic features with contemporary conveniences to produce a warm and cozy ambiance.

Enjoy a hearty prepared breakfast with regional specialties and freshly brewed coffee as you awaken. An wonderful vacation filled with genuine Sicilian experiences is guaranteed by the kind and accommodating hosts, who are always available to provide insider advice and recommendations.

Bed & Breakfast Palazzo Mazzarino: Classic Elegance
B&B Palazzo Mazzarino is the perfect option for travelers looking for a fusion of classic elegance and modern comfort. This bed and breakfast, housed in an exquisitely preserved noble mansion from the 18th century, provides a window into Palermo's colorful history. After a long day of visiting the city, guests can unwind in the room's generous space and tastefully combined old furniture and modern conveniences.

Enjoy a filling breakfast buffet that includes a variety of regional delicacies and homemade pastries. The attentive team shares their expertise of Palermo's hidden treasures and extends a warm Sicilian welcome in an effort to ensure a personalized and unforgettable stay.

B&B Casa Orioles: Peace in the Natural World

The B&B Casa Orioles offers a tranquil escape surrounded by nature on the outskirts of Palermo. This beautiful bed and breakfast offers a calm retreat from the busy city center because it is tucked away in the verdant countryside. Views of the lovely garden or the surrounding hills are included in the thoughtfully decorated rooms and suites, which provide a warm and welcoming ambiance.

Spend your mornings indulging in a sumptuous breakfast made with fresh, regional ingredients, and your afternoons relaxing by the outdoor pool or discovering the neighboring hiking trails. You will get a personalized experience thanks to the welcoming and accommodating hosts, who make this charming rural haven seem like home.

A Special Stay at a Bed and Breakfast in Palermo

Bed & breakfasts in Palermo are a wonderful alternative to conventional hotels because they give visitors a more individualized and private experience. These lodgings encourage visitors to immerse themselves in Palermo's distinctive beauty and embrace the warm hospitality of the inhabitants, from tucked-away gems in the historic center to serene getaways in the countryside. A delightful stay filled with local flavor and individualized treatment is what Palermo's bed and breakfasts provide, whether you're looking for ancient elegance, rural serenity, or modern comfort.

Hostels

O ffers a variety of lively hostels that welcome tourists on a budget and provide comfortable lodging and a welcoming environment. These affordable choices offer a great starting point for discovering the city's rich history, vibrant culture, and alluring beauty while mingling with other tourists from all over the world.

Home away from Home: Hostel Agata

In the core of Palermo's historic district, Hostel Agata provides budget tourists with a warm and comfortable setting. This welcoming hostel offers dormitory-style rooms with cozy bunk beds and communal restrooms. The common rooms are lively and welcoming, offering places for mingling, unwinding, and swapping travel tales. Enjoy the shared kitchen where you may cook your own meals or participate in group dinners the staff of the hostel hosts. The friendly and helpful staff members are always willing to share insider information about the top area restaurants, activities, and events.

In Palermo, Hostel Agata is a well-liked option for backpackers and lone travelers looking for a place to call home away from home because of its welcoming environment.

Beachside Atmosphere at Sunrise Hostel

Sunrise Hostel offers a beautiful location only meters from the lovely Mondello Beach for guests looking for a seaside experience. This relaxed hostel offers a variety of accommodations, including private rooms and dorm rooms, all of which are created with comfort in mind. Sit back and unwind in the common rooms, which include a sizable lounge and a shared kitchen, or catch some rays on the hostel's terrace.

The accommodating staff plans frequent social gatherings and outings that let visitors meet other tourists and experience Palermo's exciting nightlife. For travelers looking for a low-cost place to stay in Palermo, Sunrise Hostel provides a distinctive and memorable experience with its coastal setting and laid-back environment.

The charming urban Balarm Hostel

Balarm Hostel, located in Palermo's hip Kalsa area, mixes urban charm with a pleasant ambiance. This chic hostel offers contemporary dorm-style rooms with cozy beds and communal amenities. The communal spaces are created with a modern flair and offer spots for unwinding, mingling, and sipping a cup of regional coffee.

Utilize the complimentary city guides and maps provided by the hostel to learn about Palermo's hidden attractions. The knowledgeable and welcoming staff are always willing to share their ideas for the top local eateries, pubs, and tourist attractions. Budget tourists who want to experience Palermo's artistic and bohemian side frequently choose Balarm Hostel because of its lively community atmosphere.

An inexpensive journey around Palermo's hostels

For those who want to experience the city without breaking the bank, Palermo's hostels provide a cheap and exciting lodging choice. These hostels offer cozy beds, helpful staff, and a variety of services to guarantee a wonderful stay, whether you're looking for a sociable atmosphere, a coastal hideaway, or an urban experience. Hostels in Palermo are an affordable journey where you can meet other visitors, immerse yourself in the city's lively culture, and make lifelong memories.

Holiday rentals

Vacation rentals are a great choice for anyone wanting a more flexible and intimate stay in Palermo. These lodgings offer all the conveniences of home, enabling guests to experience local life while discovering the city's rich history, vibrant culture, and mesmerizing beauty. Palermo vacation rentals come in a variety of styles and price ranges, ranging from quaint flats in the city's historic district to chic villas by the sea.

City Center Apartments: A Convenient Location with Old World Charm

Staying in a wonderful holiday apartment will allow you to fully experience Palermo's historic district. These carefully chosen apartments provide quick access to the city's famous sites, hopping markets, and exciting nightlife since they are tucked away in the city's winding streets. You may enter Palermo's rich history and stunning architecture by simply walking outside your door.

The nicely decorated apartments provide with contemporary conveniences, making them a handy and pleasant home base for your adventures. Enjoy the freedom to prepare your own meals in a kitchen that is fully equipped, or just unwind after a day of sightseeing in the comfortable sitting room. Living in a city center apartment enables you to take in the genuine pace of Palermo's everyday life while also taking use of the comforts of home.

Villas by the Sea: Peace and Coastal Beauty

Consider renting a villa by the sea in Palermo if you're searching for a more tranquil and coastal experience. These lovely homes provide a tranquil refuge away from the city center and offer stunning views of the Mediterranean. Enjoy your morning coffee on a private balcony while listening to the sound of the sea as you awaken. The villas' elegant interior design and contemporary conveniences provide for a relaxing stay.

Explore the neighboring beaches, indulge in delectable seafood, or simply laze around in the warm Sicilian sun during the day. Palermo's seaside villa rentals provide a special chance to combine the city's cultural attractions with the peace and quiet of a coastal escape.

Retreats in the countryside: rustic charm and unspoiled beauty

Vacation villas on the outskirts of Palermo offer a dreamy retreat for those looking for a more rural and rustic experience. Stay in a classic farmhouse or a rural cottage amidst rolling hills, olive trees, and vineyards. You may get back in touch with nature and appreciate life's slower pace at these places since they provide a serene and peaceful environment. Enjoy the delights of authentic Sicilian food while exploring the scenic countryside and stopping by nearby vineyards. A rural retreat rental in Palermo offers a special chance to get in touch with the area's natural beauties and learn about the real rural way of life.

Make Yourself at Home in a Vacation Rental in Palermo

The ability to experience Palermo like a local is made possible by the vacation rentals in the city, which offer a cozy and individualized alternative to conventional lodging. You can immerse yourself in Palermo's rich culture, history, and natural beauty whether you choose to stay in a city center apartment, a beach estate, or a rural retreat. Make yourself at home in one of Palermo's vacation rentals and take advantage of the independence and adaptability that come with self-catering accommodations while making priceless memories.

Chapter 9

Practical Information

I
t's crucial to have access to useful information that
will make it easier for you to get around Palermo if
you want to make sure that your vacation there runs
well and without incident. This guide gives you the
required information to make your stay in Palermo hassle-
free, from transportation choices to important services.

Safety Advice

Even though Palermo is a typically secure location, it's
always crucial to put your own security first and take the
appropriate safety measures while there. You can guarantee
a safe and worry-free stay in Palermo by paying attention to
these safety recommendations.

- Be Aware of Your Environment: Be aware of your
  surroundings and keep your situational awareness
  up, especially in busy places, on public
  transportation, and at tourist attractions. Keep an
  eye on your possessions and keep pricey stuff

hidden if you don't want them to draw unwelcome attention.

- Use authorized taxi stands or recognized ride-hailing services when using taxis or other forms of transportation, and always make sure they are licensed. Avoid taking rides from strangers or using unmarked taxis.

- Protect Your Valuables: Always keep your valuables, such as your wallet, passport, and electronic devices, secure. Use a secure bag or a money belt that is worn close to your body. When available, keep valuables in hotel safes.

- Use ATMs with caution: Pick machines that are close to busy, well-lit places when taking out cash from them. Protect your PIN number and keep an eye out for any shady behaviour near the machine. Use ATMs located inside banks or other safe institutions wherever possible.

- Dress Properly: When visiting religious sites, especially, respect local norms by dressing modestly. You can avoid unwanted attention and demonstrate cultural awareness by doing this.

- Stay Connected: Store a copy of your identification, passport, and emergency contact information in a secure location. It's also a good idea to have a way to communicate in case of crises, such a local SIM card or access to dependable Wi-Fi.

- Research and Plan Your Itinerary: Prepare your itinerary in advance, taking into consideration transportation options, dependable tour providers, and suggested destinations. This will make it easier for you to go around the city and prevent you from getting lost in strange places.

- Trust Your Instincts: When making judgments, trust your gut and exercise common sense. Remove yourself from any situation that makes you feel uneasy or unsafe and call the police or other authorities in your area for help.

- Emergency Contact Information: Maintain a list of emergency phone numbers, including those for the local police, the embassy or consulate of your nation, and the front desk of your lodging. You'll always have access to the help you need in the event of crises or unforeseen circumstances.

You can have a wonderful trip to Palermo by being cautious and paying attention to these safety advice. Keep in mind that the key to securing a secure stay in any destination you visit is being prepared and attentive.

Local traditions and manners

Learn the norms and etiquette of the community before visiting Palermo to ensure a polite and authentic experience. You may strengthen your relationships with the people and improve the quality of your trip by being aware of and respectful of the cultural traditions of the city. Here are some important customs and etiquette pointers to bear in mind while visiting Palermo.

1. Politeness and Salutations: In Palermo, salutations play a significant role in social relations. When meeting someone for the first time, it's polite to shake their hand and make eye contact. When entering stores, restaurants, or other institutions, be sure to say "buongiorno" (good morning/afternoon) or "buonasera" (good evening). When addressing someone, it is customary to use their title (e.g., "Signore" for Mr. and "Signora" for Mrs.).

2. Dressing Properly: Palermo, like many Italian cities, values modesty and appropriate clothes, especially while seeing sacred sites or more traditional neighborhoods. When entering churches or other sacred buildings, it is recommended that you cover your knees and shoulders. Dress cleanly and respectfully in most circumstances, but feel free to adopt the easygoing, carefree Mediterranean look.

3. Table manners: Palermo is no exception to the rule that Italians take their meals seriously. It's usual to wait until everyone at the table has been served before starting to eat when dining out. Remember that while leaving a little gratuity as a sign of appreciation is customary in Italy, it is not required. Verify if the bill include a "coperto" charge that pays for bread and table service.

4. Respect religious customs: Palermo has a strong religious tradition, so you might run into different religious festivals and processions all year long. During these occasions, be respectful by acting quietly and reverently. Be aware of any warnings or guidelines regarding photography, talking, or attire when visiting churches.

5. Siesta Time: It's important to note that some businesses in Palermo still adhere to the traditional siesta time, a period of rest in the afternoon. Some businesses, offices, and services may be temporarily closed during this period, which typically occurs between 1:00 PM and 4:00 PM. Plan your activities accordingly and take this opportunity to eat a leisurely lunch.

6. Learn a Few Italian Phrases: Even though many Palermitans speak English, it will be greatly appreciated if you make an effort to learn a few fundamental Italian idioms. The Italian words "grazie" (thank you) and "prego" (you're welcome) are simple greetings that go a long way in establishing respect and creating relationships with the locals.

7. Personal Space and Queuing: Compared to certain other cultures, Italians are less formal when queuing. Don't be surprised if people stand closer to one another in lines or if people have slightly different ideas about personal space. You can go through congested spaces with easily if you have patience and a kind disposition.

8. Strike Up a Conversation: People from Palermo are renowned for their warm personalities. In a café, market, or while taking in the sights of the city, don't be afraid to start a discussion or make small talk with a local. Italians value sincere connections and take pleasure in imparting their local expertise and thoughts.

You'll not only demonstrate respect for the city's traditions by adhering to local customs and etiquette in Palermo, but you'll also improve your overall cultural experience. Keep in mind that integrating yourself into the culture can help you make deep connections with Palermitans and make new acquaintances.

Useful Phrases

While many locals in Palermo can communicate in English, learning a few basic Italian phrases will greatly enrich your experience and help you connect with the city and its people on a deeper level. Here are some useful phrases that will come in handy during your stay in Palermo:

Greetings:
- Buongiorno - Good morning/afternoon
- Buonasera - Good evening
- Ciao - Hello/Goodbye (informal)
- Arrivederci - Goodbye

Politeness:

- Per favore - Please

- Grazie - Thank you

- Prego - You're welcome

- Scusa - Excuse me

- Mi scusi - Excuse me (formal)

- Mi dispiace - I'm sorry

-

Introductions:

- Come ti chiami? - What's your name? (informal)

- Come si chiama? - What's your name? (formal)

- Mi chiamo... - My name is...

- Piacere di conoscerti - Am glad to meet you (informal)

- Piacere di conoscerla -Am glad to meet you (formal)

Ordering Food and Drinks:

- Vorrei... - I would like...

- Un caffè, per favore -Please, a coffee,

- Un bicchiere di vino rosso/bianco - A tumbler of red/white wine

- Il conto, per favore -, Please,the bill

Directions:

- Dove si trova...? - Where is...?
- A sinistra - On the left
- A destra - On the right
- Dritto - Straight ahead
- Vicino - Near
- Lontano - Far

Asking for Help:

- Mi può aiutare, per favore? - Can you help me, please?
- Non capisco - I don't understand
- Può ripetere, per favore? - Can you repeat, please?
- Mi sono perso/a - I am lost

Basic Numbers:

- Uno - One
- Due - Two
- Tre - Three
- Quattro - Four
- Cinque - Five

- Dieci - Ten

Common Expressions:

- Che bello! - How beautiful!
- Mi piace molto - I like it very much
- Mi scusi, dov'è il bagno? - Excuse me, where is the restroom?
- Mi potrebbe consigliare un ristorante? - Could you recommend a restaurant?
- Che ora è? - What time is it?

Remember, even attempting to speak a few basic Italian phrases shows your willingness to engage with the local culture and will be appreciated by the people of Palermo. Don't be afraid to make mistakes, as the locals are often patient and encouraging. Enjoy your linguistic adventure in Palermo!

Emergency Contacts

While Palermo is generally a safe city, it's always important to be prepared and have access to emergency contacts in case of any unforeseen situations. Whether you need immediate medical assistance, report a crime, or require other emergency services, here are the essential contact numbers to keep in mind during your stay in Palermo:

Emergency Services:
Police Emergency: 113
Medical Emergency: 118
Fire Department: 115

Tourist Police:
Polizia di Stato - Sezione Turistica e Antirapina: +39 091 605 8017
This specialized unit of the police force assists tourists and provides information regarding safety, lost items, and other non-emergency concerns.

Embassy and Consulate Contacts:

It's advisable to note down the contact details of your country's embassy or consulate in Palermo. They can provide assistance in case of passport issues, emergencies, or other consular services.

Pharmacies:

Farmacia (Pharmacy) - Look for a green cross sign, which indicates a pharmacy. Pharmacies in Palermo generally operate during regular business hours. In case of emergency medication needs outside these hours, there are 24-hour pharmacies available in the city. Ask your hotel or accommodation provider for the nearest 24-hour pharmacy information.

Hospital:

Policlinico Universitario - This is the main hospital in Palermo, equipped to handle emergency medical situations. In case of a medical emergency, it's recommended to call the emergency number (118) for immediate assistance and guidance.

Lost or Stolen Documents:

If you lose your passport, identity documents, or credit cards, contact your embassy or consulate immediately for guidance on reporting the loss and obtaining a replacement.

General Safety Tips:

Palermo is a relatively safe city, but it's always wise to take precautions. Be mindful of your belongings and avoid displaying expensive jewelry or valuables in public.

Use licensed taxis or reliable transportation services, and avoid unmarked or unofficial vehicles.

When exploring at night, stick to well-lit and populated areas.

If you encounter any suspicious activity or feel unsafe, don't hesitate to seek assistance from local authorities or ask for help from nearby establishments.

Remember, emergency situations can be stressful, but having these important contact numbers readily available will help you handle any unexpected events with confidence.

CHAPTER 10

Palermo Travel Itineraries

Here are some well prepared travel itineraries that will help you make the most of your stay in Palermo, whether you have a few days or a week to spend there: These travel itineraries give you a taste of the many interesting things Palermo and its surroundings have to offer. You are welcome to alter these itineraries in accordance with your interests and the amount of time you have available.

Never forget to immerse yourself in the community's culture, enjoy the mouthwatering cuisine, and experience the welcoming Sicilians. Palermo will leave you with priceless memories of your Sicilian experience because to its interesting history, beautiful architecture, breathtaking scenery, and mouthwatering cuisine.

Palermo for a Day

You may still enjoy the essence of this bustling location if you just have one day to visit the beautiful city of Palermo.

A well-planned schedule is provided below to help you make the most of your stay in Palermo:

Morning:

- Visit the stunning architectural wonder that is the Palermo Cathedral first thing in the morning. Admire its minute features and discover its rich past.

A short stroll will bring you to the Palazzo dei Normanni, where you may tour the magnificent Palatine Chapel and take in the splendor of this ancient palace.

Explore the thriving markets in Ballar or Vucciria, where you can stroll through busy streets lined with colorful stalls selling local specialties, fresh produce, and one-of-a-kind crafts. Enjoy some genuine street food while soaking up the bustling environment.

Afternoon:

- After a delectable meal of street cuisine, proceed to Albergheria's old area. Explore the area's winding lanes, take in the stunning architecture, and stop by the Church of San Cataldo, which is renowned for its distinctive Arab-Norman design.

Discover the fascinating Church of San Giovanni degli Eremiti, known for its tranquil cloister and crimson domes.

Go for a leisurely stroll through the lovely Palermo Botanical Garden (Orto Botanico di Palermo), where you can get away from the busy city and take in the tranquil beauty of nature.

Evening:

- Make your way to Teatro Massimo, one of Europe's biggest opera theatres, as the day draws to a close. Take advantage of the chance to see the splendor and cultural significance of this historic theater by attending a play or a guided tour, if they are offered.

You can enjoy a delicious meal at a neighborhood trattoria where you can sample typical Sicilian delicacies to cap off your day. Don't pass up the opportunity to sample some Sicilian sweets, such cannoli or cassata, as a delightful way to end your trip to Palermo.

Even though one day may seem brief, this schedule enables you to visit some of Palermo's most famous sites, immerse yourself in its bustling markets, and sample its distinctive cuisine. Don't forget to take your time, take in the scenery, and enjoy the charm of this amazing city.

Palermo for three days

The ideal time to explore Palermo's rich history, vibrant culture, and architectural marvels is if you have three days to spare there. Here is a carefully thought-out schedule to help you maximize your three-day stay:

Day 1: Ancient Palermo

- Start your adventure by visiting the magnificent Palermo Cathedral, where you may marvel at its imposing grandeur and detailed embellishments. Explore its chapels and crypt at your own pace.

- Visit the majestic Palatine Chapel at the Palazzo dei Normanni. Admire the magnificent mosaics and tour the royal rooms to gain an understanding of the city's regal past.

Experience the energetic ambiance of the Ballar Market. Spend some time getting lost in the maze of tiny alleyways, taking in the atmosphere, and enjoying some authentic Sicilian street food.

- In the late afternoon, take a trip to the peculiar and slightly unsettling Palermo Capuchin Catacombs. Explore the unsettling underground chambers containing mummified remains that provide a window into Palermo's history.

Day 2: Culture and the Arts

- One of Europe's largest opera theaters, the Teatro Massimo, should be your first stop of the day. Explore its lavish interiors and discover its interesting history by going on a guided tour.

- Visit the Galleria d'Arte Moderna in the charming Kalsa area to learn about the modern art scene.

Enjoy the wide variety of modern and contemporary paintings.

- Visit the Museo Archeologico Regionale, a regional archaeology museum that is home to an extraordinary collection of ancient Sicilian antiquities.

Enjoy a leisurely stroll along Foro Italico's waterfront promenade while taking in expansive views of the city skyline and the sea.

Day 3: Relaxation and Gardens

- Spend the morning strolling through the lovely Palermo Botanical Garden (Orto Botanico di Palermo). Explore its magical passageways to find uncommon plant species and take in the tranquility.

- Go to the Zisa Castle, a magnificent illustration of Islamic-Norman design. Explore the surrounding grounds while admiring the lovely decor.

- Travel to Mondello, a quaint beach village. Take a stroll along the golden sand beach, cool down in the sparkling seas, and savor some fresh seafood at a waterfront restaurant.

Take a leisurely stroll through Palermo's exquisite shopping boulevard, Via della Libertà, which is studded with shops and cafes, in the evening.

This three-day itinerary will give you the chance to discover Palermo's well-known landmarks, dig into its intriguing history, and become fully immersed in its dynamic culture. Spend some time enjoying the regional cuisine, mingling with the amicable residents, and making memories of your trip to this alluring Sicilian city.

Seven days in Palermo

You have plenty of time in Palermo with seven days to thoroughly immerse yourself in the city's rich history, savor its culinary treats, and travel outside its walls to explore the surroundings. Here is a thoughtful itinerary to help you make the most of your seven-day stay:

Day 1 Highlights: Arrival and Palermo

- Start your journey with a walking introduction of Palermo's historic district. Discover the bustling markets in Ballar or Vucciria, take in the magnificent architecture of the Palermo Cathedral and the Palazzo dei Normanni, and take in the energetic energy of the city.

- You can enjoy regional favorites like arancini, panelle, and cannoli at a nearby trattoria where you can treat yourself to a classic Sicilian dinner.

Day 2: Cefalù and Monreale

- Visit the magnificent Monreale Cathedral on a day trip to Monreale. From the mountaintop, marvel at its brilliant mosaics and take in the expansive views of Palermo.

- Travel onward to the quaint seaside village of Cefalù. Visit the impressive Cefalù Cathedral, stroll through its charming streets, and unwind on the lovely sandy beach.

Day 3: Segesta and Erice

- Take a day excursion to Segesta to explore the ancient Greek theater and temple that are surrounded by beautiful scenery.

- Visit the hilltop village of Erice, renowned for its magnificent vistas and medieval buildings.

- Visit the Venus Castle, stroll around its winding streets, and have some delectable almond pastries.

Day 4: The Neighborhoods of Palermo

- Investigate Palermo's several neighborhoods, including Kalsa, Albergheria, and La Vucciria. Explore their neighborhoods, go to old churches and palaces, and eat at secretly excellent restaurants to sample the regional fare.

- Experience Palermo's exciting nightlife in the evening by listening to live music or going to a cultural event.

Day 5: Valley of the Temples and Agrigento

- Visit the spectacular Valley of the Temples in the historic town of Agrigento during a day trip. Explore the well-preserved Greek remains and take in the ambiance of the past.

Day 6: Marsala and Mozia

- Visit the Marsala region, which is known for producing Marsala wine. Visit a nearby wincry and indulge in wine tastings there.

- Continue on to the island of Mozia, which is home to interesting Phoenician history and old ruins. To get to the island and discover its historical riches, take a boat journey.

Day 7: Relaxed and Goodbye

- Relax on one of Palermo's stunning beaches, like Mondello or Cefalù, on your last day there. Take in the sun, beach, and sea while you cherish your remaining time in Sicily.

- In the evening, enjoy a special supper honoring the delights of Sicilian cuisine as you say goodbye to Palermo.

The finest of Palermo and its surroundings, from its fascinating historical monuments to its picturesque scenery and delectable cuisine, can be experienced during this seven-day journey. Accept the Sicilian way of life, take your time to get to know the people, and make lifelong memories that you will love.

CONCLUSION

The city has a mesmerizing fusion of rich history, cultural gems, and delectable cuisine. This city has much to offer any traveler with its stunning architecture, lively markets, and comfortable Mediterranean environment. Palermo delivers a rich and fascinating experience, whether you choose to explore its historical sites, indulge in its delectable cuisine, or travel outside its limits for spectacular day trips.

Visit famous sites like the Palermo Cathedral, the Palazzo dei Normanni, and the Teatro Massimo to immerse yourself in the city's unique history. Explore the vivid markets like Ballar and Vucciria, where a sensory feast of flavors and colors from regional foods and street cuisine is created. Enjoy the active nightlife of the city, which offers live music, cultural events, and lively clubs and pubs.

Explore the surrounding areas on day outings to places like Monreale, Cefalù, Segesta, and Agrigento. These outings give visitors the chance to discover historic sites, charming coastal villages, and beautiful natural settings, deepening their awareness of Sicily's rich cultural history.

Palermo provides a variety of lodging choices to satisfy the needs of every visitor. There are accommodations to suit every taste and budget, from opulent hotels and homey bed and breakfasts to inexpensive hostels and chic vacation rentals.

The bustling food scene in Palermo is a highlight of any trip there. Enjoy authentic Sicilian cuisine, fresh fish, as well as sweet treats like gelato and pastries. Visit the city's cafes, bars, and pubs to relax with a cup of espresso or a glass of reviving local wine.

Palermo has its own norms and etiquette, so it's crucial to be aware of them as you move around the city. For a worry-free journey, familiarize yourself with the city's transit alternatives, comprehend the currency and money exchange procedure, and make a note of emergency contact information.

Whether you're a history buff, a foodie, or a voracious traveler, Palermo guarantees an amazing trip. This city encourages you to immerse yourself in its distinctive attractions, from its intriguing landmarks and hidden gems to its warm and inviting attitude. Pack your luggage, preheat your appetite, and get ready to travel through Palermo's heart and soul, where traditional practices and contemporary delights coexist harmoniously.

Recommendation

Look no further than Palermo if you're looking for a place that mixes history, culture, and delectable cuisine. This vivacious Sicilian city has a wide range of experiences that will fascinate you and leave you wanting more. Here are some tips to make your trip to Palermo better:

Immerse Yourself in History: View the Palermo Cathedral, Palazzo dei Normanni, and Teatro Massimo, three magnificent buildings in the city. To properly understand the significance of these landmarks, take guided tours or investigate the interesting history behind them.

Dive Into the Local Cuisine: Sample the arancini, cannoli, and other traditional Sicilian foods. In the lively marketplaces of Ballar and Vucciria, you may indulge in street food and take in the local cuisine.

Explore the world beyond Palermo by taking advantage of day trips to adjacent places. Visit Cefalù for its lovely alleys and stunning beaches, or go to Monreale to behold the magnificent mosaics of the cathedral there. For their historic ruins and breathtaking scenery, Segesta, Agrigento, and Erice are other worthwhile exploration destinations.

Explore the Palermo neighborhoods by taking a stroll through Kalsa, Albergheria, and La Vucciria to get a feel for the neighborhood's culture. Visit hidden beauties, talk to welcoming residents, and sample regional cuisine at nearby eateries.

Take use of Palermo's lovely parks, gardens, and beaches to engage in outdoor activities. There are many outdoor activities to enjoy, such as tanning at Mondello, hiking in the nearby natural reserves, and engaging in water sports along the coast.

Take Advantage of the Exciting Nightlife: Enjoy the exciting ambiance of Palermo's bars, taverns, and live music venues. Participate in the pleasure by consuming regional wines and beverages while dancing to traditional Sicilian music.

Offering Accommodations for Every Taste: Depending on your interests and budget, pick from opulent hotels, quaint bed & breakfasts, or cheap hostels. If you want to be close to the main attractions, think about staying in the city center; if you want a tranquil getaway, consider a beach resort.

Embrace Local Customs: Acquire a basic command of the Italian language to converse with people and to respect their traditions. Engage the amiable Sicilians and enjoy their gracious hospitality.

Palermo's rich history, diverse cuisine, and picturesque surroundings all contribute to its attraction. It's a place that will forever etch itself into your heart and provide lifelong memories. So get ready to enjoy Sicilian culture and be enchanted by Palermo's charm. Your journey lies ahead!

Made in United States
Orlando, FL
24 August 2023

36370152R00122